FACE TO FACE

FACE

TO

FACE

INTERVIEWS WITH

CONTEMPORARY

NOVELISTS

edited by ALLAN VORDA

introduction by DANIEL STERN

RICE UNIVERSITY PRESS *Houston, Texas*

Request for permission to reproduce material from this work
should be addressed to

Rice University Press
Post Office Box 1892
Houston, Texas 77251

Book design by Patricia D. Crowder

LIBRARY OF CONGRESS CATALOGING-IN-PUBLICATION DATA

Vorda, Allan, 1948–
    A conscientious recorder : interviews with contemporary novelists /
    Face to Face interviews with contemporary novelists / Allan Vorda.
        p. cm.
    Includes index.
    ISBN 0-89263-322-0 :
    1. American fiction—20th century—History and criticism—Theory,
etc. 2. Novelists, American—20th century—Interviews. 3. Fiction—
Technique. I. Title.
PS371.V67   1993
813'.5409—dc20   93-11347
                                                             CIP

Several of the interviews have appeared in similar form in the
following publications: *Extrapolation*, Fairleigh Dickinson University
*Literary Review, Michigan Quarterly Review, Mississippi Review,
New Letters, Sonora Review, Writers and Their Craft.*

Photography credits: Kazuo Ishiguro by Nigel Parry, Max Apple by
Jerry Bauer, Cristina Garcia by Scott Brown, Jamaica Kincaid by
Mariana Cook, Ron Hansen by Julie Hansen, Marilynne Robinson by
Jerry Bauer, Robert Stone by Michael A. Smith, Hubert Selby, Jr., by
K. C. Baley.

For three women in my life

Ruth "Bob" Redmond
Patricia Redmond Vorda
Le-My Nguyen Vorda

Contents

Acknowledgments

I would like to thank my mother, Patricia Vorda, and my sister, Patty Robinson, for their help with this book. They provided many hours of secretarial help and the use of their word processor to make these interviews presentable.

My thanks also to the following editors: Tom Unger/ *Sonora Review* (Ron Hansen interview); Laurence Goldstein/*Michigan Quarterly Review* (Max Apple interview); James McKinley/*New Letters* (Max Apple interview); Donald Hassler and Joanna Hildebrand/*Extrapolation* (Greg Bear interview); Rie Fortenberry and Frederick Barthelme/*Mississippi Review* (Jamaica Kincaid, Robert Stone, and Kazuo Ishiguro interviews); Walter Cummins and Jill Kushner/*Literary Review* (Hubert Selby, Jr., interview).

Introduction

The literary interview has become a pervasive part of the contemporary literary landscape. I stress contemporary as distinct from modern. A rough guess of the phenomenon's age might be, perhaps, thirty years.

Try to imagine, for example, Ezra Pound interviewing T.S. Eliot on the complex process of revising "The Waste Land"—and then being rebuffed when he tries to elicit from Old Possum the intimate origins of that poem in Eliot's painful first marriage—the confessional shape of a fairly typical literary interview of today. After all, the two great poets were friends and literary confreres, together engaged in the thrilling adventure of literary modernism. Yet, impossible as it is to imagine then, it is *not* hard to imagine today, so ubiquitous is the interview culture in which we live. That imaginary interview did not, could not have happened, for one simple reason. Because the nature of the private creative process and the line between the autobiographical and the invented has been, for generations now, blurred. Into the no-man's land occupied by that blurring has entered the Literary Interview.

Eliot's famous dictum about the writer's urge to escape from personality must read like ancient Greek to today's writers and readers. In fact, the odyssey of the literary interview in our time has been very much a struggle between issues of personality and questions of craft.

It is to some extent the tension between those two poles

of interest that gives the form its energy and sustains our interest.

This said, it is useful to note that the literary interview has been traditionally employed as an imprimatur, a kind of cap to reputation—a piece of the fame that writers work toward, coming in the fullness of a career—the magisterial *Paris Review* series Writers At Work, which began with E.M. Forster and continues to the present day, being the classic paradigm.

If that is the "classic" mode, then the liveliness of the book at hand may come from its nature as a kind of revisionist treatment. It carries interviews with writers whose reputations are just barely beginning, as in the case of Cristina Garcia. It presents names almost faded, as with Hubert Selby, Jr. It tracks rising reputations, as with Ron Hansen, and allows itself to be dazzled by comet-like re-known, as with Kazuo Ishiguro. In addition we have, in effect, an interview with a genre: literary science fiction, represented by Greg Bear, a genre too often left out of serious literary consideration. Rounding out the unconventional vision of the book, we are given an interview with a kind of underground hero, Max Apple, whose *Oranging of America* is a hidden classic of American comic vision, but one that is long out of print.

Here we see that the literary interview may do the work of discovery and rediscovery instead of merely supporting literary celebrity, may perform the work of defining a career in progress as well as simply eliciting the truths of craft from Mount Olympus.

It may seem strange to include interviews with Cristina Garcia and Marilynne Robinson, each of whom has published one novel, along with Robert Stone who, in mid-career, is an iconic figure in American fiction. However, the fact of their inclusion reminds us that the "peak-of-career" model is not the only useful one.

Garcia, for example, in her interview, overtakes the area

traditionally assigned to the novel. It brings us to what Samuel Butler called "news from nowhere." As a first-generation Cuban who left the island at the age of two, she exercises a special authority in describing the assimilation of magical realism into her otherwise very New York novel, *Dreaming in Cuban*.

Marilynne Robinson, whose novel *Housekeeping* has had a career all its own as a book and a film, tells us that "I couldn't have written *Housekeeping* if I hadn't had children." And her justification of that remark has remarkable resonance—especially to women.

Another point of difference in *Face to Face* is the mixing of foreign and domestic, and the almost-forgotten and the hot commodity. Hubert Selby, Jr.'s *Last Exit To Brooklyn* was an electric publishing event almost thirty years ago. And of course Kazuo Ishiguro became instantly famous in 1989 with the publication of *The Remains of The Day* (qualifying both for the foreign and the hot commodity), the result being a bridge of loosely strung ideas, evasions, technical discussions, and personal/literary histories—a bridge that spans oceans, races, and decades.

In almost every one of these interviews, the question of Identity arises in a serious way. Both Ishiguro and Jamaica Kincaid take startling, unpredictable positions regarding the ethnic links to one's background. And, of course, the very presence in this book of an ethnic Japanese, a native from Antigua, and a Jew from Grand Rapids, Michigan, makes one realize how different such a book might have looked, say, in 1928. It would most likely have included Hemingway, Fitzgerald, Cummings, Sinclair Lewis, and Virginia Woolf. These rebels all were nevertheless children of a homogeneous culture. In our splintered contemporary world, the literary community sings its song in many tongues, and in harmonies undreamed of by previous generations.

The particular pleasures this collection of interviews offers us are the result of its content and its fortunate structure. It becomes more than a sum of its parts, and the stage is set for unplanned, happy accidents of consonance. Robert Stone and Ron Hansen both discuss the relevance of Joseph Conrad to their own very different styles. John Gardner's controversial theses in *On Moral Fiction* keep coming up, are attacked, defended, and elucidated. Jamaica Kincaid and Cristina Garcia share a love-hate response to the lands of their birth.

As the writers talk to each other over the shoulder of the interviewer, we are, after all, happy eavesdroppers on Mount Olympus. Craft, art, sexuality, theology, pop culture, masturbation, nationalism: nothing human is alien to these artists and their art. And we are the beneficiaries of their open and complex confessions.

But their final and finest gift to readers is to return us to the books we read, changed in the way we see the art and techniques of fiction. Perhaps, best of all, closing the book we will begin to see connections between the telling of stories and the living of lives we have not seen before.

Robert Stone says it best: "All I'm trying to do is lead people to something they already know."

Still, while on the surface the literary interview appears to be a voluntary, pleasant encounter for both parties, it may not be quite that simple. There is, often, a fair amount of aggression and counter-aggression hidden beneath the exchange of Q and A. At heart, one senses that the literary interview may be, in many ways, an adversarial relationship. It is the interviewer who wields a prod—and the probing is often deflected and corrected by evasions of the writer at hand.

Even the trivial questions asked of writers at parties, irritating in social life, can yield illuminating results in the context of the literary interview. "Was thus-and-so character based on someone in your personal experience?" One wants, irrationally, to know that Robert Cohn in *The Sun Also Rises* is based on Hemingway's friend Harold Loeb.

But it is not entirely idle information. Once we learn that Hemingway could paint such a harsh portrait of a "friend" we have moved a step closer to understanding Hemingway's complicated attitude toward friendship. (Loeb helped Hemingway publish his first stories; to help Hemingway was to ensure his turning on you later, as Scott Fitzgerald discovered and as Ford Madox Ford would have learned had he been alive when *A Moveable Feast,* with its scabrous portrait of him, was published.)

It is also possible to learn from such portraiture how the author goes about excluding certain aspects of the "model's" reality just as art criticism goes about its studies in Picasso and Matisse. Thus, merely by examining one supposedly trivial and gossipy question, one can see how much there is to learn. The same could undoubtedly be said for banal questions such as, "How do you write? On a computer, a typewriter, standing up at a desk, lying in bed like Rossini?" Properly examined, the idlest of questions and the most evasive of answers can shed special light on the creative process—as within the texture of fiction itself, the possibility of surprising swerves lurks in every exchange.

Only look at Kazuo Ishiguro's response to Allan Vorda's question about his extraordinary and swift "success." The author, in his characteristically controlled way, traces the British literary world's response to the combination of a super-British subject—an aging butler's view of his proto-fascist employer—and a Japanese name and face on the book jacket. Reading beneath the text, one finds here an anger at what might be called a kind of reverse racism. The British have rewarded Ishiguro for being a Japanese who has taken for himself the Kipling/Forster/Waugh tradition—and given it a sly twist. The reader suspects that Ishiguro is both pleased at his success and furious at the patronizing attitude implied in it. All presented, of course, with Ishiguro's typical leashed irony.

Thus, the form of the literary interview proves that there

are no trivial questions. One analogy that suggests itself is that of analyst and patient. All questions are objective, yet all questions are loaded explosives that may go off if they touch hidden fire.

Some years ago the *Paris Review* asked me to do an interview with Bernard Malamud for their series Writers at Work. Malamud had refused all overtures from the magazine for more than a decade. Then, on the occasion of his sixtieth birthday, he relented. However, he insisted that the interview be conducted by a friend, myself. Clearly, Malamud viewed the interview situation as a potential occasion for aggression and misunderstanding. I sent him the final transcript of the interview. (The *Paris Review* has always allowed their subjects to review the results and make changes.) When it came back, considerably transformed— reading in places like a piece of writing by Malamud— there was a question added that I never thought to ask.

PR: What is the source of *The Assistant?*
BM: Source questions are piddling, but you're my friend, so I'll tell you.

Perhaps the ultimate response to feeling helpless in the hands of the interviewer is to imagine your own questions and write your own reply—taking charge of "piddling" questions by creating them and then responding.

We live in the midst of a critic's war on the author, a time when we are being encouraged to see literature in terms of a "readerly" text, when the critical eye is all and the author's role is being deconstructed into nonexistence. In this context, the literary interview may be seen to take on a new value. Here the interviewer deconstructs the author-as-text; and the author illuminates, beguiles, distracts, evades, and from time to time confesses. He may even, on occasion, rebel, may strike back and deconstruct the interview-as-process.

All this said, the strategies of art do not easily yield themselves to the inquiring ear, eye, and mind. In these matters no one ever has the last word. But Henry James may have come closest when he wrote in "The Middle Years": *"We work in the dark—we do what we can—we give what we have. Our doubt is our passion and our passion is our task. The rest is the madness of art."*

—DANIEL STERN
New York City
1993

Stuck on the Margins

AN INTERVIEW WITH

Kazuo Ishiguro

K<small>AZUO</small> I<small>SHIGURO</small> was born in Nagasaki, Japan, in 1954, and emigrated to Britain in 1960. He attended the University of Kent at Canterbury and received an M.A. in creative writing from the University of East Anglia. In 1982 he was included in the original "Best of Young British Novelists" after having become a British citizen earlier that year. He is the author of three novels, and each has received a literary award: *A Pale View of Hills* was awarded the Winifred Holtby Prize by the Royal Society of Literature in 1982; *An Artist of the Floating World* won the 1986 Whitbred Book of the Year Award; and *The Remains of the Day* won the Booker Prize in 1989, Britain's top literary award. He currently lives in London with his wife, Lorna MacDougall, and their daughter.

The interview with Kazuo Ishiguro occurred on April 2, 1990, in Houston, where the author was a guest of the Houston International Festival. (Additional questions were provided by Kim Herzinger of the *Mississippi Review*.) Originally, we were to conduct the interview in his hotel downtown, but when I arrived Ishiguro seemed restless. Courteously, he asked if the interview could be conducted somewhere else, since he had been cooped up in his hotel for three days. We drove to my house in Sugarland, a sprawling suburb southwest of Houston, and conducted the interview in the kitchen, with Ishiguro talking and sipping ice water. As we talked, I studied his face with its broad Oriental planes and features and listened to his very clipped British accent, a startling juxtaposition—at first. During the course of the interview, I came to realize that this was an extraordinary young writer with a tremendous understanding of his craft. At the end of the interview, Ishiguro asked if we could have a late lunch of Mexican food since he never could find it in England.

KH: Last year, just before you went back to Japan for the first time since you left at the age of six, you were somewhat worried that the Japanese would expect you to know a great deal more about the culture and the country than you actually did. Were your fears realized?

KI: Not really. It's partly because they knew I was coming. I had a very kind of closeted journey to Japan. I was invited by the Japan Foundation, which is part of the government, so there was always an escort hanging around. In fact, there was far more media interest in me than I had anticipated. I caused a great stir in the press— not because they were particularly interested in me as a literary figure—but because I touched a *strange nerve* from the social aspect. Japan is, at the moment and perhaps for the first time, facing the idea that they cannot remain a homogeneous society.

This question about immigrants from Southeast Asia as well as a greater number of Western people living in Japan has started up a process. They now have to start thinking about what it means to be Japanese and what sort of country Japan might be. This has suddenly become a live-wire issue. This idea that somebody who is racially Japanese and looks very Japanese could go to England and have lost his Japaneseness in some ways is at the same time fascinating and I think rather threatening. So there was all this interest in what kind of person I was and what messages I could bring and what the West thought about Japan. They somehow thought that I was somebody they could actually ask. So I found myself put in that sort of false territory there.

I was on TV and I did a lot of interviews and things—but very rarely about literature. There were always these questions about what do people think of Japan and what did I think of Japan.

AV: Did you respond in Japanese?

KI: No, I spoke English all the time and I was advised to do so. Really just to avoid this confusion—that was my way of saying I'm not a regular Japanese guy. My Japanese isn't good enough anyway to speak correctly. I could make myself understood, but in Japan that is not enough. There are about seven or eight different ways to say the same thing depending on how you perceive the status of the person you are speaking to, vis-à-vis yourself. To get this kind of thing even slightly wrong produces tremendous offense. It's a terribly hierarchy-conscious society, although, in a curious way, it is a classless society. It means people aren't worrying about whether they are upper class or middle class or working class. They are worrying about what number they are on the ladder.

AV: Did the people there like the answers you gave them, or did your answers increase their xenophobia?

KI: I avoided giving any clear-cut answers, but I think just my very being is a kind of embodiment of the whole issue.

A lot of Japanese are starting to properly travel for the first time, and by this I don't mean just as tourists. Business and international trade means that they are spending more time abroad. Of course, they have children who are growing up abroad. This is something that some people say is good and others say is horrifying because their Japaneseness is going to become dissipated. The fear is that these people and their children will come back to Japan having lost something, such as eating with chopsticks, which is part of the cultural tradition.

A lot of the younger Japanese, particularly in Tokyo, know very little about things that people in the West consider to be traditionally Japanese. They don't even know how to put on the kimono. (I suppose I would be a good example since I don't know.) If you do it the wrong way around—the left on the inside or the right on the outside or whichever way it is—it's a terrible blunder because one way you only do to a corpse; living people have it the other way, and I never can remember which way it is. But what was interesting is a lot of the young Japanese don't know because they don't wear kimonos and they don't know a lot of the basic things. The younger kids, particularly in Tokyo, are kind of like Western kids in that sense. It is a kind of baffling, weird thing from a bygone era.

They also eat meat all the time. I was shocked at how tall they were as well. Anyone under thirty is six or seven inches taller on average than anyone over thirty. This is partly due to eating American junk food, so, of course, they may not live as long.

The older Japanese are small, but they live a long time. I think they still have the longest life expectancy in the industrialized world, although sometimes the Scandinavian countries compete in this area.

Thus, the whole trip was interesting and I think it's the way the world is going now since we're becoming much more international. America has always had this melting pot reputation, and now Britain has to face up to the question of multiculturalism. The Japanese are beginning to realize it's going to be their turn since Japan is the last large industrialized country that hasn't yet faced this problem.

AV: You stated in the *New York Times Book Review* that,

"Publicity for me has to a large extent been fighting the urge to be stereotyped by people." Do you think the stereotyping is due to your ethnicity and to the fact that your first two novels were set in Japan?

KI: There is a kind of paradox about my books being set in Japan and whether this stereotypes me or not. In Britain, around the time when I published my first novel, the climate had actually turned toward a great deal of interest in writers who wrote books set in that particular setting. I think there was a very peculiar thing going on in Great Britain at that time. I tend to think if I didn't have a Japanese name and if I hadn't written books at that stage set in Japan, it would have taken me years longer to get the kind of attention and sales that I got in England with my first two books. What happened in Britain, certainly during the time when I was at university, contemporary fiction was, I won't say dead, but it seemed to be the preserve of a very small strata of a very small British society. We all had this image of contemporary British novels being written by middle-aged women for middle-aged middle-class women.

Some of them are good and some of them are appalling, but that wasn't one of the exciting things that was happening when I was growing up. Anyone interested in the creative arts was interested in theater. There was a whole explosion with a kind of radical theater. Rock music, cinema, and even television—because we have quite serious arts television in Great Britain—were the kind of things that everyone was talking about while the novel had a kind of sleepy, provincial, cozy, inward-looking kind of image and no one was interested in it.

Around 1979 and 1980 things changed very rapidly. There was a whole new generation of publishers and a whole new generation of journalists who came of age at that time, and they desperately wanted to find a new generation of writers to rediscover the British novel. I think there was something wider going on in English society at that time, too. There was an awareness that Britain was a more international place, a more cosmopolitan place, but it wasn't the center of the world. It was kind of a slightly peripheral, albeit still quite wealthy, country. It started to be aware of its place within the context of the whole international scene. In the early 1980s there was an explosion of tremendous interest in literature that suddenly appeared almost overnight. This occurred in foreign-language literature with people like García Márquez, Milan Kundera, and Mario Vargas Llosa, who became very trendy people. At the same time, there was a whole generation of younger British writers who often had racial backgrounds that were not the typical white Anglo-Saxon. Even some of the "straight" English writers were also using settings or themes that tend to be international or historical. So there definitely was this atmosphere where people were looking for this young, exotic—although exotic may be somewhat of an unkind word—writer with an international flavor. I was very fortunate to have come along at exactly the right time. It was one of the few times in the recent history of British arts in which it was an actual plus to have a funny foreign name and to be writing about funny foreign places. The British were suddenly congratulating themselves for having lost their provincialism at last.

The big milestone was the Booker Prize going to Salman Rushdie in 1981 for *Midnight's Children*. He previously had been a completely unknown writer. That was a real symbolic moment, and then everyone was suddenly looking for other Rushdies. It so happened that around this time I brought out *A Pale View of Hills*. Usually first novels disappear, as you know, without a trace. Yet I received a lot of attention, got lots of coverage, and did a lot of interviews. I know why this was. It was because I had this Japanese face and this Japanese name and it was what was being covered at the time.

I tend to think I got a very easy ride from the critics. I subsequently have won literary prizes with each book, which is very important in Britain, career-wise. It's one of the things that help you climb the ladder. All these things sort of happened to me, and I think it greatly helped that I was identified as this kind of person.

Yet, after a while, this became very restricting, and the very things that helped me in the first place started to frustrate me as an artist and as a serious writer. I don't want to be confined by these things even though they were quite helpful publicity-wise.

KH: In Britain there is a rather large community of extremely important and active writers who come from, or often write about, cultures quite different from the English, Irish, Scottish, and Welsh. I'm thinking of V.S. Naipaul, Salman Rushdie, William Boyd, Lisa St. Aubin de Teran, Doris Lessing, Ruth Prawer Jhabvala, and even Americans like Paul Theroux, David Plante, and Russell Hoban. Do you find yourself grouped with them often? Do you mind it? Do you resist it? Do you think such a grouping is of any use in coming to grips with your work?

KI: Like any writer, I resist being put in a group. The group you mentioned there is quite an eclectic one. I'm usually put in a much more narrow group—usually with Rushdie and a writer called Timothy Mo, who probably isn't that well known in America.

He's a Chinese-British writer who is quite prominent in Britain and has been nominated for the Booker Prize twice. He hasn't won it yet.

I write so differently than someone like Rushdie. My style is almost the antithesis of Rushdie's or Mo's. Their writing tends to have these quirks where it explodes in all kinds of directions. Rushdie's language always seems to be reaching out—to express meaning that can't usually be expressed through normal language. Just structurally his books have this terrific energy. They just grow in every direction at once, and he doesn't particularly care if the branches lead nowhere. He'll let it grow anyway and leave it there, and that's the way he writes. I think he is a powerful and considerable writer.

I respect Rushdie's writing enormously, but as a writer I think I'm almost the antithesis. The language I use tends to be the sort that actually suppresses meaning and tries to hide away meaning rather than chase after something just beyond the reach of words. I'm interested in the way words hide meaning. I suppose I like to have a spare, tight structure because I don't like to have this improvised feeling remain in my work. From a literary point of view, I can't see anything that links me with someone like Salman Rushdie or Timothy Mo.

If we can generalize at all about these writers, I think there is something that unites most of the writers that you have mentioned, especially the younger writers of Britain at the moment. There is something different about them, if you compare that group with the older generation of writers of Britain. The one possible, valid thing that unites the younger group is the consciousness that Britain is not the center of the universe. There was a time when Britain thought it had this dominant role in the world for a long time, that Britain thought it was the head of this huge empire. I think for a long time it was supposed you could just write about British issues and about British life and it would automatically be of global significance, since people all around the world would be interested. British writers didn't have to consciously start thinking about the interests of people outside Britain, because whatever concerned them was, by definition, of international interest.

I think there was this gray period—because literary habits take a long time to die—before the British finally, both intellectually and consciously, had accepted that the empire had gone. No longer did they have this dominant, central place in the world to go to anymore. I think perhaps the styles of writing and the assumptions of writing took a while to catch up with that, and I think this was rather a dull period in English writing. The writers were writing things in which nobody was interested, since it meant nothing to anyone outside of Britain; yet, they carried on with the assumption that Britain was the center of the world. In fact, it was this that turned it into this provincial little country.

I think the younger generation of writers not only realized that, but are now suffering from a kind of inferiority complex. There's a great sense that the front line where the great clashes of ideologies were happening was elsewhere. So whether you are looking at communism and capitalism clashing or the Third World and the industrialized world clashing or whatever it is—people have this idea if you're actually based in Britain and British life is what you know—then you have to make some sort of leap. Either you go out there physically and start searching around as V.S. Naipaul and Paul Theroux did, or you have to use your imagination. It's much more normal for the younger generation of British writers, and, apart from the people you mentioned, I would also include Julian Barnes and Ian McEwan, that they will very often not write books in the contemporary British setting they live in. They will search far and wide in their imaginations for mythical settings or historical settings. For example, McEwan's novel *The Innocent* is set in the Cold War period of Berlin. This is not atypical of the differences that separate the younger generation from the older generation of writers.

KH: Americans like to believe that English language literature somehow became theirs after World War II. We pay some lip service to Greene, Golding, Lessing, Amis, Fowles, Larkin, Heaney, Hughes, Powell, Murdoch, and the rest, but not much. In fact, I would say that Americans half feel that English literature never quite recovered from the deaths of Joyce and Woolf and the war itself. How do you see yourself, and other young contemporary British writers, in terms of the twentieth-century tradition of British writing?

KI: What I just said previously raises questions about style and technique as well as setting and theme. If you happen to actually live in a country that you think won't actually provide a broad enough setting to address what you see as the really crucial issues of the age, that inevitably means you start moving away from straight realism.

If you happen to be, let's say, living in East Germany at the moment, perhaps there's no overwhelming reason to not write realism. I think there's a natural instinct to write realism. It takes much more to start thinking of other ways to write. It's when you are actually *stuck on the margins*. Then you start to become conscious that you are stuck on the margins and the things that you know intimately on that concrete, documentary level just won't do. Yet, on the other hand, you realize you won't have the same authority as someone who lives in Eastern Europe, or someone who lives in Africa, or the Soviet Union, or America to write about the places that you think are rather central to the things you would like to talk about. What can you do? You know about English life and the texture of English society, but it's something you feel you can't use that well. So you start to actually move away from realism. You have to start looking for other ways in which to work. I think here you start to move, not so much into out-and-out fantasy, but you start to create a slightly more fabulous world. You start to use the landscape that you do know in a metaphorical way. Or you start to create out-and-out fantastic landscapes. Perhaps Doris Lessing got caught up in that when she went off on her science fiction venture.

It may well be that Americans are going through some of the stages that British writers once went through because American society is today so central to the world community. What are the international themes that are of interest to everybody? In America there is no need to ask this question consciously. Americans are almost exempt from having to ask that question. Perhaps they shouldn't be. In any case, at this moment, I think people can write about American society and American life and it will be of interest to people in Kuala Lumpur or the Philippines because American culture has a broad appeal. It has gotten to the point that some people say American culture is invading or taking over everywhere you go in the world. Thus, a lot of people are trying to stop it, but a lot of people are bringing it in. It's very difficult to think of any point on the globe—or any society in the world today—where people shouldn't have a valued interest in American culture.

For the time being, just because of the way things are, I think American writers find themselves in this position— that they can write in a way that at other times might seem very inward-looking and parochial. Just by virtue of America's cultural position in the context of international culture, American writers are going to be relevant. So writers who haven't tried to be of great interest to people all over the world end up being so, sometimes precisely because they're so inward-looking and unconscious of the world beyond, and they reveal so much about where a lot of these influences are coming from. I think there was a time when British writers were in this position. Perhaps American writers need to be aware of a time when it will no longer be the case for them.

AV: Do you see your prose as participating in the more traditional, twentieth-century style of such writers as W. Somerset Maugham, E.M. Forster, Evelyn Waugh, and Joyce Cary?

KI: Not really. Most of them I haven't even read. With *The Remains of the Day* it's like a pastiche where I've tried to create a mythical England. Sometimes it looks like or has the tone of a very English book, but actually I'm using that as a kind of shock tactic: this relatively young person with a Japanese name and a Japanese face who produces this extra-English novel or, perhaps I should say, a super-English novel. *It's more English than English.* Yet I think there's a big difference from the tones of the world in *The Remains of the Day* and the worlds created by those writers you mentioned because in my case there is an ironic distance.

AV: Maybe I misread you somewhat. Are you saying that readers have to get past the realism in order to reach—as Barth or Borges or García Márquez have termed it—the irrealistic or fabulist world? This is more of your intent with *The Remains of the Day* than just writing a traditional British novel?

KI: Absolutely. I think it's almost impossible now to write a kind of traditional British novel without being aware of the various ironies. The kind of England that I create in *The Remains of the Day* is not an England that I believe ever existed. I've not attempted to reproduce, in a historically accurate way, some past period. What I'm trying to do there, and I think this is perhaps much easier for British people to understand than perhaps people abroad, is to actually rework a particular myth about a certain kind of England. I think there is this very strong idea that exists in England at the moment, about an England where people lived in the not-so-distant past, that conformed to various stereotypical images. That is to say, an England with sleepy, beautiful villages with very polite people and butlers and people taking tea on the lawn.

Now, at the moment, particularly in Britain, there is an enormous nostalgia industry going on with coffee table books, television programs, and even some tour agencies who are trying to recapture this kind of old England. The mythical landscape of this sort of England, to a large degree, is harmless nostalgia for a time that didn't exist. The other side of this, however, is that it is used as a political tool—much as the American Western myth is used here. It's used as a way of bashing anybody who tries to spoil this Garden of Eden. This can be brought out by the left or right, but usually it is the political right who say England was this beautiful place before the trade unions tried to make it more egalitarian or before the immigrants started to come or before the promiscuous age of the '60s came and ruined everything. I actually think it is one of the important jobs of the novelist to actually tackle and rework myths. I think it's a very valid ground on which a novelist should do his work. I've deliberately created a world which at first resembles that of those writers such as P.G. Wodehouse. I then start to undermine this myth and use it in a slightly twisted and different way.

I was asking you earlier on, and this is a question I ask a lot of American people who know American literature, about the genre of the Western myth. It's always puzzled me that serious writers have not to a greater extent tried to rework that myth because it seems to me a nation's myth is the way a country dreams. It is part of the country's fabulized memory, and it seems to me to be a very valid task for the artist to try to figure out what that myth is and if they should actually rework or undermine that myth. It has happened in the cinema as far as the Western is concerned, but when I ask this question people don't seem to be able to offer many serious literary works that go into that area.

To a certain extent, I suppose I was trying to do a similar thing with the English myth. I'd have to say that my overall aim wasn't confined to British lessons for British people because it's a mythical landscape which is supposed to work at a metaphorical level. *The Remains of the Day* is a kind of parable. Yet this is a problem I've always had as a writer throughout my three books. I think if there is something I really struggle with as a writer, whenever I try to think of a new book, it is this whole question about how to make a particular setting actually take off into the realm of metaphor so that people don't think it is just about Japan or Britain. Because ultimately I'm not that interested in saying things about specific societies; and, if I were, I think I'd prefer to do it through nonfiction and follow all the proper disciplines such as to actually produce evidence and argument. I wouldn't do it by emotional manipulation.

AV: Perhaps it is less interesting to do it through nonfiction because it is less imaginative. I guess that is one of the joys of writing fiction.

KI: I think one of the joys of fiction is that you are actually saying things that are universal and not just about Great Britain or America or whatever. It can be about America or Britain, but I think when fiction really takes off it is because you can actually start to see how it is relevant to all other kinds of contexts and how there is a universal streak to these things. I always have this real problem because, on the one hand, you have to create the setting in your novel that feels firm enough, concrete enough, for people to be able to find their way around it. On the other hand, if you make it too concrete and too tied down to something that might exist in reality, that fictional work doesn't take off at that metaphorical level and people start saying, "Oh, that's what it was like in Japan at a certain time," or, "He's saying something about Britain in the 1930s." So, for me, it is something that I feel I haven't quite come to terms with yet, but I'm trying to find some territory, somewhere between straight realism and that kind of out-and-out fabulism, where I can create a world that isn't going to alienate or baffle readers in a way that a completely fantastic world would—but a world which, at the same time, can actually prompt readers to say that this isn't documentary or this isn't history or this isn't journalism. I'm asking you to look at this world that I've created as a reflection of a world that all kinds of people live in. It's the movement away from straight realism that is actually the real challenge. You get that wrong and you could lose everything, whereby no one identifies with your characters or they don't care what happens in this funny, weird, bizarre world. I just wanted to somehow move it away so it's just a couple of stages from straight realism in order to let it take off with that metaphorical level. I think I've come closer to doing that in *The Remains of the Day* than I did with the two Japanese novels, but I still feel this is a challenge I have to meet.

AV: Your prose is a joy to read. For example, on page twenty-seven of *The Remains of the Day* you write: "I was then brought up to this room, in which, at that point of the day, the sun was lighting up the floral pattern of the wallpaper quite agreeably." And shortly thereafter, the butler Stevens thinks that the "greatness" of Britain paradoxically comes from "the lack of obvious drama or spectacle that sets the beauty of our land apart." Can the same analogy be made to your writing style?

KI: When Stevens says that about the British landscape he is also saying something about himself. He thinks beauty and greatness lie in being able to be this kind of cold, frozen butler who isn't demonstrative and who hides emotions in much the way he's saying that the British landscape does with its surface calm: the ability to actually keep down turmoil and emotion. He thinks this is what gives both butlers and the British landscape beauty and dignity. And, of course, that viewpoint is the one that actually crumbles during the course of Stevens' journey.

To a large extent, when I wrote *The Remains of the Day*, that was the first time I started to become very conscious of my own style. And, of course, quite rightly, these references that Stevens makes are also a reference to my own style. I think what happened was this. My first two novels I just wrote these sentences without really thinking about style. I was just writing in what I thought was the clearest way possible. Then I started to read review after review which talked about my understated or clipped style. It was the reviewers and the critics who actually pointed this out to me—where my style seemed to be unusually calm with all this kind of strange turmoil expressed underneath the calm. I actually started to ask myself, "Where does this style come from then?" It's not something I consciously manufactured. I had to face the possibility that this was actually indeed something to do with me. It's my natural voice. In *The Remains of the Day,* for the first time, I started to question to what extent that was a good or bad thing from the human point of view regarding this whole business about the suppression of emotion.

Perhaps this was actually revealed by this style, by this inner voice, that I produced in my first two books. To a certain extent, *The Remains of the Day* actually tackles on a thematic level the implications of that kind of style. Of course, Stevens' first-person narrative is written in that style, but of course his whole life is led in that style. And in the book I try to explore to what extent it is indeed dignified and to what extent it is a form of cowardice—a way of actually hiding from what is perhaps the scariest arena in life, which is the emotional arena. It is the first book I've written in which I was actually conscious of my own style and to a certain extent tried to figure out what it is and why it's like that and where it's coming from.

KH: Despite a comparatively paltry audience in the United States, there is a feeling that you, along with Ian McEwan, William Boyd, Martin Amis, Salman Rushdie, Julian Barnes, Graham Swift, and a few others—plus the inter-

national success of *Granta*—are leading an energetic new
wave in English fiction. How does it seem to you?

KI: It is very hard for me to assess what is going on in
America because I have just visited, but it does surprise
me the extent to which the Atlantic does seem to be this
huge gap between the two literary cultures. There are
household names here that aren't even available on the
bookshelves in Britain and vice versa.

When I came over here to do my tour with Knopf in
November, I discovered that there were these people who
are literary giants here. For instance, consider Ann Beattie, who I don't think is readily available on the bookshelves in England. You might be able to track down a
copy of an Ann Beattie book, but you could talk to a lot
of literary journalists in London and they would not have
heard of her. Quite likely they would not have heard of
Russell Banks. On the other hand, Raymond Carver has
become very well respected in England, as has Richard
Ford. I would say these two writers have broken through
to significant respect and readership in Britain.

All the time I'm coming across books here that I realize
are very well known over here, but quite often these
names mean very little to me. I've been given a book by
Pete Dexter called *Paris Trout*, which I think is quite a
well-known book here and I've noticed he's won the
National Book Award. Personally, I had a hell of a time
breaking through here. I don't know why there should be
this huge gap, but I think it just points to the fact that—
even though we share the same language—the literary
cultures are so different.

The other factor has to do with the actual publishing
industries, because so much of publishing has to do with
contacts and literary politics. I think one of the real
weaknesses of the system as it operates at the moment is
that there is a tendency toward insularity. If you start
operating any contact games then the mediocre domestic

talent is always going to get promoted over more interesting stuff from abroad.

KH: Since you studied American literature at university,
were there any American writers who influenced your
work? I hear that you think Hemingway, for instance,
wrote great titles, but that perhaps the books that followed were a bit of a letdown.

KI: I think Hemingway did write marvelous titles. I like
Hemingway's early work, but I find some of his later stuff
pretty mediocre, almost embarrassingly so, but his standard of title writing remained high right to the end. I
think *Across the River and Into the Trees* is a marvelous
title, but the discrepancy between the quality of the title
and the book is one of the greatest discrepancies I've
come across in world literature. It is staggering someone
who could write a title like that could write such an
appalling book, but he did write some fine stuff early on.

   With American writers I tend to like the older guys
from the nineteenth century, such as Mark Twain. I think
Huckleberry Finn is a very beautiful book with a real
liveliness to the language and the vernacular is very exciting. *Moby Dick* is a crazy book, yet very interesting. I like
Edgar Allan Poe, who raises some very interesting questions about literature as a whole.

AV: What about contemporary American writers such as
Pynchon, Gass, and Barth?

KI: These are all people that I should say that we don't
really read in England. Pynchon is read. . .well, I don't
know. . .he is bought. Usually the only book of his that
anyone has read is *The Crying of Lot 49*, because it's
short. A lot of people possess *Gravity's Rainbow* and *V.*,
but I know very few people who have gotten over one-
third of the way through. It remains to be seen if people
will finish *Vineland* in England, but people are buying
him. Pynchon may very well be a very important writer,
but I've only read *The Crying of Lot 49*, so I'm not in a

position to say. From what I've read, it is a little too over-intellectualized for me. I suppose one of these days I should tackle his big novels.

AV: I can't think of one writer in America who gets more critical attention than Pynchon.

KI: Perhaps he is a great writer, or it could be because there will always be a certain kind of writer who is good for academics.

AV: Can you name one thing that separates American literature from British literature?

KI: One feature of your literary scene here that we don't have in Britain and generally in Europe is the creative writing industry. I think that is one of the enormous differences in the two literary cultures. It's probably true to say, and I've heard it often said, that you can't find a single American writer today of any significance who hasn't in some way been directly touched by the creative writing world, either as teacher or student. Even someone who kept away from it is going to be affected by it indirectly, because so much of the criticism and so much of the opinions of his fellow writers are going to be touched by it. I think this is something that would certainly make me nervous if I were living in a literary culture where the role of the universities and faculties who taught creative writing began to have that sort of dominant influence.

I'm not actually suggesting that the Thomas Pynchon phenomenon is something closely related to this, because I'm not in a position to comment on him. All I would say is that I would want to assess quite carefully what the role of the creative writing faculties actually is within the whole literary culture because, whether you like it or not, American literature is going a certain direction because of this and I would want to determine if the influence were benign or whether it was actually leading us up a garden path.

KH: Lately in this country there has been some debate over the virtues of fictional "minimalism" *(Granta* called it "dirty realism")—Raymond Carver, Ann Beattie, Frederick Barthelme, Max Apple, Mary Robison, Richard Ford, Tobias Wolffe, and a number of others have been called "minimalists." Readers seem to like the work, but it has sent critics into spasms of concern over the death of the novel, the end of American fiction, and so on. Do you have any thoughts on the subject? Is there anything like minimalism and the subsequent outcry from the critics in contemporary British writing?

KI: No. There isn't a compatible movement or phenomenon in British writing at all. Minimalism isn't a word that you hear very often in British literary debate. I should say in relation to the previous question that Richard Ford and Raymond Carver are two American writers that I admire enormously. Raymond Carver is a profoundly moving writer while Richard Ford has written two or three short stories that are amongst the finest short stories I've ever read. Perhaps it is the influence of the creative writing industry that somehow led to that sort of style, but if that's the case, then that is an aspect that I'll be quite well disposed toward because I think those two writers write with great emotional honesty about things that strike me as being genuinely deep at the human level.

The thing I fear from the creative writing industry and universities in general is that people elevate priorities that I would not consider to be terrifically important. They'll elevate to some special status issues like the nature of fiction or some rather cerebral intellectual ideas. Such issues become esteemed in that kind of environment because, after all, that is what that kind of environment celebrates. But, for me, while the nature of fiction or fictionality are things that writers might need to be concerned with to get on with their work, I don't believe that the nature of fiction is one of the burning issues of the late twentieth century. It's not one of the things I want to turn to novels and art to find out about. I think reading Ford and Carver for me is a kind of an antidote really to those over-intellectualized or self-conscious literary creations that almost seem to be created for the professor down the corridor to decipher. Carver and Ford seem to write about life in a way that is profound. Also, at the technical level, I think they are in a different league from a lot of these people who are just trying to show off or make comments about their literary techniques. The technique applied by Ford or Carver is one at the highest level and to the point that perhaps it's not that obvious. I think they say great things about the emotional experience of life.

Minimalism is not something that is discussed very much in Britain. Short stories haven't really caught on in Britain recently. You can bring out a volume of short stories and you know that only about one-third of the people read it, as opposed to the number of people who read a novel that you have written. For some reason the British don't get into short stories.

KH: To what extent has Japanese fiction influenced your work? If we look around for writers who sound a bit like Ishiguro, it would seem that Tanizaki—especially his cool precision and delicate touch—is closer to you than anybody else.

KI: Tanizaki wrote in various different styles, and a lot of his books I wouldn't describe as cool or delicate. I think the book that is best known in the West is one called *The Makioka Sisters*. It is really like a Western family saga. It is one of those stately, long books like Henry James, Edith Wharton, Theodore Dreiser, or George Eliot would have written. It's about this rich merchant family where nothing terribly dramatic ever happens, but it follows the different family members through a period of social change. I think a lot of people think that Tanizaki always writes

like that, but he also writes kind of weird, kinky, perverted stuff.

AV: What book would you be referring to?

KI: *The Secret History of the Lord of Musashi*, which is
about a medieval lord who, the first time he gets sexually
turned on, is wandering around a battlefield shortly after
a battle and he sees these severed heads. I think that night
he peeks through a hole and sees some women dressing
the severed heads of fallen clan members and he starts to
get sexually turned on.

AV: I'm sure Freud would have had a good time with this.

KI: It gets even weirder because the thing that really turns
him on is a particular head that has a nose missing. So
when he becomes a powerful lord later on, he has a real
sexual craving for severed heads with missing noses. It
gets really funny because there is a particular guy that he
takes a liking to and he really wants to see this guy
without a nose and so he keeps trying to arrange it so that
his nose will get cut off, but it never quite works. This
poor guy doesn't know what the hell is going on. Every
few weeks he loses an ear or something happens to him,
or somebody is after him, but he doesn't know why.
There is this weird scene where the lord gets his servant
to impersonate a severed head without a nose while he is
making love to one of his concubines.

I mean, this is real Tanizaki territory, and this is where
Tanizaki is really interesting. And there are a few other
books like that. This is, by way of saying, that there is this
tendency, just because I have a Japanese name, to pull out
one or two other Japanese writers somebody else has
heard of and say there is a similarity to my writing. Yet
the critic perhaps is basing this comparison to a Japanese
writer whose book is not typical of others he has written.
For example, Tanizaki wrote in a lot of different styles
and he wrote for a long, long time. Tanizaki actually
went into his eighties, and he produced an enormous

amount of books as he went through lots of different stages. I can't really see that anybody would particularly compare me to any Japanese writer if it weren't for the fact that I have this Japanese name. Now if I wrote under a pseudonym and got somebody else to pose for my jacket photographs, I'm sure nobody would think of saying, "This guy reminds me of that Japanese writer." I often have to battle and to speak up for my own individual territory against this kind of stereotyping. I wouldn't say it's wildly unfair, but then I can think of a dozen other writers with whom I could just as easily be compared. I would say I am not wildly dissimilar to the Tanizaki of *The Makioka Sisters,* but then someone could equally say that for anybody almost—whether it was George Eliot or Henry James or the Brontë sisters.

KH: How about Chekhov? He would seem to be the one overwhelming influence on American writing over the past ten to fifteen years.

KI: Chekhov is a writer that I always acknowledge as one of my influences. When people ask me about the writers I really like, I always say Chekhov and Dostoyevsky.

To backtrack just slightly on my refuting any affiliation with Japanese literature, there are some things I have learned from the Japanese tradition, if you like, but perhaps more from the Japanese movies. I think it is the same thing that perhaps I've taken from Chekhov, and that's from reading these people and seeing movies by film makers like Ozu and watching the plays of Chekhov and reading Chekhov's short stories. I think it's given me the courage and conviction to have a very slow pace and not worry if there isn't a strong plot. I think there is an overwhelmingly strong tradition in Western literature— at least I should say British literature and American literature since I think the French have a slightly different thing going—in which plot is pretty important. By fiction I also mean movies and the way television stories are told and so on. It is almost assumed that plot has to be the central spine around which the story is fleshed, and that is almost the definition these days. When you actually think about Chekhov, it is really rather hard to actually see his pieces as plots with flesh on it. What is interesting is in Japan, until very recently, this kind of plot-with-flesh model just didn't exist in Japanese fiction.

There are writers like Kawabata, whom I find quite baffling and alienating, because he's from such a different tradition, but at the same time fascinating because he writes kind of long short stories. I believe he is the only Japanese Nobel Prize winner for literature. Kawabata's stories are often completely plotless. They are not only plotless, but the pace goes so slowly sometimes it almost stops. These things seem to break all the rules people teach about how to write screenplays for Hollywood.

This business about pace, you read these books on how to write a screenplay or books on how to keep the narrative drive going, yet reading Chekhov or some of these Japanese writers has indicated that you don't have to worry about that very much. I've really started to get into this idea of slowness with things almost stopping.

AV: This seems evident in *The Remains of the Day* where the plot is loosely based; yet, you are able to piece things together. For example, Miss Kenton disappears for much of the novel, but she is always there when you need her to pull things together. The use of Miss Kenton's character seems to allow you to intermingle different elements.

KI: I don't structure my books around plots, and I find it a great liberation. If you have to worry about making a plot work, you often have to sacrifice other priorities to the mechanical workings of the plot, and you start to distort characters and all kinds of psychological insights. I find a great deal of freedom in not having plot, but that does actually mean you have to face lots of new challenges about not boring the reader and how to structure your work. These are some of the things in Chekhov which I find a continual revelation. How does he keep you absorbed when all the people are doing is just sitting around a field and asking whether or not they are going back to Moscow? He should be crushingly boring. In fact, one or two of those great plays *are* boring, but some of his short stories are masterpieces.

AV: Which ones in particular?

KI: It's probably not that well known, but I like "Ionych." Other stories that come to mind are "A Boring Story," "Lady with Lapdog," and "The Kiss."

AV: You stated after you wrote *A Pale View of Hills* that, "If you really want to write something, you shouldn't bring things into your book lightly. It's a bit like taking in lodgers. They're going to be with you a long time. I think the most important thing I learned between writing the first and second novels is the element of thematic discipline." Do you now feel you have control of your thematic discipline after having written *The Remains of the Day?*

KI: I'll never say I've got control, but I think I've gotten more and more control with each book. When I read reviews, I've always read the opening and closing paragraphs to see if they're saying this is good or not so good, but then after that the next thing that concerns me is the summary. Have they actually summarized the book in the way that I wanted the book to come over? For a long time, at the beginning of my career, I would actually get favorable reviews that praised me for a book that I didn't wish to write. They were emphasizing all the wrong things and praising me for things I didn't intend to do. So I could keep quiet about it and accept unwarranted praise. Of course, this isn't very satisfying, and the question of thematic discipline comes in here. There is a real satisfaction to be gotten from being praised for exactly the right things you wanted to be praised for and not for some accidental effect you created. Because that is what you're trying to do. You're not just trying to get people to like your book—you're trying to communicate a vision. This is why thematic discipline is so important to me. I used to read all these reviews recommending that people should read my first book for the weirdest reasons, but it had nothing to do with what I was wanting to do. I was pleased because they were favorable reviews, but that was a very frustrating experience for me.

The one point I still feel an element of frustration about, and I mentioned this before, is that people have a tendency to say that *The Remains of the Day* is a book about a certain historical period in England or that it is about the fall of the British empire or something like that. They don't quite read it as a parable or see it take off into a metaphorical role. Now, a lot of reviewers have understood my intent and said this is not just a book about a butler living in the 1930s. It is interesting that reviews vary from country to country. It tells you something about that country, but it also reminds you that as a writer you're going to be read by lots of different people in lots of different social contexts coming at the book from lots of different directions. I think it's always a healthy thing to remind oneself that you shouldn't assume every reader's assumption is going to be the same as a British reader's assumption. There are going to be very obvious reasons why some people see it in a completely different way. And usually the further I get from Britain the happier I am with the readings, because the people are less obsessed with the idea of it just being about Britain. In Britain, I suppose I'm still slightly locked into this realist reader and I recognize that a part of that is my own responsibility. I hate to use the word "fantastic," but the book is still too realistic for the metaphorical intentions to be obvious if the people actually come from the society which the book superficially resembles.

I've been very happy about the way the American reviewers, on the whole, have read *The Remains of the Day*. One or two have thought it was specifically about British history, but, by and large, most people read it the way that I intended them to. As I say, I think I had more trouble in Britain, where some people thought it was about the Suez Crisis or it was about British appeasement of Nazi Germany.

KH: *The Remains of the Day* and *An Artist of a Floating World* both seem to be about men who have an extraordinary capacity to lie to themselves while presenting themselves as very precise and cautious truthtellers. Should we imagine that this is going to be the central obsession in your work? So far, the central notions in your work would seem to demand first-person narration. Are you planning to work in any other forms?

KI: I think this is always a difficult question about how you're going to develop as a writer. I find it rather difficult to plan more than one book at a time, and I can't really say now which other themes I'm going to be obsessed about in two or three books from now. I think, certainly, what happened with my first three books is that I was actually trying to refine what I did over and over again, and, with *The Remains of the Day*, I feel that I came to the end of that process. That is why the three books seem to have a kind of similarity. It's not a similarity for which I can apologize; I have no other way of working.

I don't actually think of my writing as being an attempt to cover this territory and finish it and then move over to a different territory altogether and have a go at that. I don't see it like that. I feel like I'm *closing in on some strange, weird territory* that for some reason obsesses me, and I'm not sure what the nature of that territory is, but with every book I'm kind of closing in on this strange territory. And that's the way I see my development as a writer. Quite often I will have an idea for a story which is intrinsically quite interesting, but I know immediately that I can't use it because I know it's not going to help me close in on this territory. It has gotten to the point now that I recognize this. I know the things that apply to this territory which will be relevant or might be relevant from the ones that are quite diverting and therefore irrelevant. If I'm reading a newspaper and I come across an item, occasionally something will hit me, something that is perhaps quite banal, but it rings some kind of strange bell. The item doesn't necessarily have to be some kind of weird human interest story, because quite often some ordinary situation will just spring out from the page at me and I'll think that's something I could use.

I don't intend to write about old men looking back over their lives all the time because I think I've come to the end of that, but I think the real challenge that always faces writers is what to keep and what to cast off from their previous concerns and previous books. I think it is important to try to identify those things that still mean something to you, that still feel unfathomed in some way, and that is the way that you close in further and further on this territory. I think most writers do write out of some part of themselves—that is, I wouldn't say "unbalanced," but where there is a kind of lack of equilibrium. I'm not suggesting that writers are usually unbalanced people. I know many, many writers, and I would say that most of them are *more than averagely sane* and responsible people, but I think a lot of them do write out of something that is unresolved somewhere deep down and, in fact, it's probably too late ever to resolve it. Writing is kind of a consolation or a therapy. Quite often, bad writing comes out of this kind of therapy. The best writing comes out of a situation where I think the artist or writer has to some extent come to terms with the fact that it is too late. The wound has come, and it hasn't healed, but it's not going to get any worse; yet, the wound is there. It's a kind of consolation that the world isn't quite the way you wanted it but you can somehow reorder it or try and come to terms with it by actually creating your own world and own version of it. Otherwise, I can't see any other explanation for why people should actually do this time-consuming, antisocial activity of locking themselves away and obsessively writing. I think serious writers have to try, in some way or the other, to keep moving in a direction that moves them toward this area of irresolution and lack of balance. I think that's where the really interesting, deep writing comes from. This is partly why I'm very wary of the creative writing industry. I think it could actually deflect potentially very profound individual voices away from what their muses are trying to tell them.

AV: Please comment on such characters as Etsuko, Ono, Miss Kenton, and Stevens, who have misused their talents or have not led lives of fulfillment because of a lack of insight. And also, conversely, would their lives be better off if they had insight and no talent?

KI: I wrote about these people not actually to pass judgment on them, because I am interested in people who do have a certain amount of talent—not just talent—but who have a certain passion, a certain real urge, to do a little bit more than the average person. They've got this urge to contribute to something larger.

AV: I can see where this applies to Ono in *An Artist of the Floating World*, but do you think it applies to Stevens?

KI: Yes, definitely. Stevens is somebody who desperately wants to contribute to something larger, but he thinks he is just a butler and the only way he can do this is to work for a great man. He gets a lot of his sense of self-respect from an idea that he is serving a great man. If he were someone who didn't care at all about how his contribution was being used, then he wouldn't end up a broken man at the end. He is driven by this urge to do things perfectly, and not only do things perfectly, but that perfect contribution should be, no matter however small a contribution it is, to improving humanity. That is Stevens' position. He's not content to say, "I'll just get by and earn money so that I can feed myself."

AV: But then again, it doesn't seem that Stevens has any great insight as to why he does things. Nor does he seem to have a great understanding of the world.

KI: That's true, Stevens doesn't have a great understanding. I think this is where my characters go wrong. Their lives are spoiled because they don't have any extraordinary insight into life. They're not necessarily stupid; they're just ordinary. (I write out of this fear that I, myself, will waste my talent—not only waste my talents, but, indeed, end up backing some cause that I actually disapprove of or one that could be disastrous.) Yet, these ordinary characters often are going to get involved in a kind of political arena even if it's in a very small way. The reason I chose a butler as a starting point was that I wanted a metaphor for this vehicle. Most of us are like butlers because we have these small, little tasks that we learn to do, but most of us don't attempt to run the world. We just learn a job and try to do it to the best of our ability. We get our pride from that, and then we offer up a little contribution to somebody up there, to an organization, or a cause, or a country. We would like to tell ourselves that this larger thing that we're contributing toward is something good and not something bad, and that's how we draw a lot of our dignity. Often we just don't know enough about what's going on out there, and I felt that's what we're like. We're like butlers.

AV: You also briefly present the lives of Lisa and the footman with whom she elopes. This seems to be a microcosm of what could have been a more fulfilling or happier life if Stevens had allowed himself to fall in love with Miss Kenton instead of denying his feelings.

KI: I had this story of Lisa and the footman because I just wanted a scene where they were confronted with just such a situation and how they (Stevens and Miss Kenton) would actually talk about it and discuss it. It refers to something they're both painfully concerned with, and, yet, they have to discuss it as a kind of professional incident or setback. When Stevens is thinking back over his life, this is one of the things that comes back to him, which is the closest they ever got to discussing their romantic possibilities. So even when Stevens and Miss Kenton are discussing their unfulfilled romance, they do it indirectly by discussing Lisa and the footman.

AV: Stevens' vision is very myopic in that he never seems to give a thought to anything, nor is sex an issue. Do you agree that he is a pathetically tragic figure that is almost nonhuman in his thoughts and feelings?

KI: I wouldn't want to say nonhuman.

AV: Maybe if I could digress just one second. You had that interesting metaphor in *The Remains of the Day* where Mr. Cardinal suggests to Stevens that it might be better if people were created as plants, "firmly embedded in the soil," then there wouldn't be any disagreements about "wars and boundaries." Then Mr. Cardinal adds, "But we could still have chaps like you taking messages back and forth, bringing tea, that sort of thing. Otherwise, how would we ever get anything done?"

KI: I think he's in danger of turning himself into something less than human partly because he's got this sense of perfectionism. It's this kind of terribly misguided sense of perfectionism, which, if he actually achieves it, would actually mean turning himself into something less than human. But it's not just perfectionism. It's a kind of a cowardice. That is what I'm trying to suggest and, hence, the juxtaposition of his ambition to be a great butler with his avoidance of a romantic life with Miss Kenton. I suppose I'm suggesting that often that kind of drive to that kind of professional perfectionism is rooted in some kind of cowardice about the emotional arena. It's not just a determination to be the best. Once again, I was drawn to use a butler in this kind of metaphorical way because that seemed to be a profession in which at least a stereotypical view of the professional butler is that you have to kind of erase the obviously human from yourself. This was probably a social requirement because people wanted privacy at the same time as wanting to be served. So the butler was obliged to be a kind of robot-like figure.

AV: Nevertheless, it seems as if Stevens is devoid of any feelings. For example, his proudest moment as a butler is during Lord Darlington's political conference when his father is dying upstairs. He ignores being with his father since his duty lies elsewhere—primarily trying to get bandages for the sore feet of the snotty Dupont. Even after his father dies, Stevens does not go to attend to the corpse, whereupon Miss Kenton sarcastically says, "In that case, Mr. Stevens, will you permit me to close his eyes?" It's as though Stevens is made of cardboard, without any identity or feelings.

KI: The role of the butler is to serve inconspicuously while creating the illusion of absence and at the same time being physically on hand to do these things. It seemed to me appropriate to have somebody who wants to be this perfect butler because that seems to be a powerful metaphor for someone who is trying to actually erase the emotional part of him that may be dangerous and that could really hurt him. Yet, he doesn't succeed because these kinds of human needs, the longings for warmth and love and friendship, are things that just don't go away. This is what Stevens probably realizes at the end of the novel when he starts to get the inkling about this question of bantering. He starts to read more and more into why he can't banter, and this is an indication of the fact that he's somehow cut off from other people. He can't even make the first steps in forming relationships with other people.

AV: In the *New York Times Book Review*, you say your next book will not be repetitive stylistically and that you might "like to write a messy, jagged, loud kind of book." What kind of book can your readers expect next?

KI: It is very difficult to say. I write very slowly, and most of my writing time I'm not actually writing prose. *The Remains of the Day* took me three years and during that time I did nothing else. I don't have any other job, and I turn down any offers to do journalism. I was full-time working on that book, but I realized afterwards, looking through my diary, that I actually spent only twelve months writing the words that ended up in that book. It horrifies me to think that I spent two years just working up to it, but I find that I have to have a very close map of where I'm going to go before I actually start to write the words. I have to have it almost all in place in my head first. This is once again quite unusual, because I know plenty of writers who write brilliantly, although they know very little of where they're going when they start the first draft. I have to have all these things worked out and researched. Now things may change, obviously, in the execution, when I'm actually writing the words, but I usually have to know fairly precisely what I'm trying to achieve with every paragraph. So it takes me a long time to get to that situation. I fill folders and folders up with notes and ideas which look like excerpts from a longer work. I may experiment with a particular tone or a character during the very early stages when it's very difficult to say even where the book is going to be set. All I know are the themes.

A Continuing Act of Wonder

AN INTERVIEW WITH

Max Apple

M<small>AX</small> A<small>PPLE</small> was born October 22, 1941, in Grand Rapids, Michigan. He attended the University of Michigan, where he received several Hopwood Awards for writing, as well as his Ph.D. in English literature in 1970. Since 1972, he has taught at Rice University. Mr. Apple is a mercurial man with gray curly hair and a beard. He has published four books: *The Oranging of America* (1976), a collection of short stories; *Zip* (1978), a novel; *Free Agents* (1984), a collection of prose pieces; and *The Propheteers* (1987), a novel. He and his wife, Talia Fishman, live in Houston, Texas, with their two small daughters and his two children from a previous marriage.

The interview took place on the morning of February 19, 1987, in a third-floor office of the English Department at Rice University in Houston. Though small and dark, the office was fairly typical of those on the campus' main quadrangle: a single window afforded scholars an uninhibited view of the tomb of Rice's founder; built-in bookcases contained only dust and a few yellowing *New Yorker* cartoons; and towers of books, arranged almost deliberately around the room, caused one to wonder if the occupant was in the process of moving into or out of the office.

The taping of the interview began with the two of us sitting across from each other at a small wooden table in the center of the room.

AV: *The Propheteers*, your second novel, has just been released. When one first starts reading it is like seeing an
old friend because the first chapter is essentially the short
story "The Oranging of America." Yet there is a sense of
mistrust on the reader's part that this has been ground
already covered. By using former characters and themes,
do you feel you have opened up yourself for criticism
such as John Barth received for his epistolary novel *Letters*?

MA: Yes. I worried about that and I thought of just leaving
that out because a lot of people had read it. On the other
hand, even if people had read it before, it is still the
starting ground because you need to know who Howard
Johnson is. That was in my mind when I originally wrote
the story: I wanted it to continue. I ended it many years
ago with him about to meet the Disneys. It's just life got
in the way of finishing it. I did worry about it, I do worry
about it, and I think it's a legitimate criticism. I just have
to ask the reader's trust, assuming some readers will have
read it, that their curiosity will equal mine to see what
happens.

AV: Later on you also incorporate the short story "Walt
and Will" (from *Free Agents)* for chapters seventeen and
eighteen. By now the reader can see you are weaving an
intricate fabric utilizing American characters of almost
mythic proportions. Did it coalesce as early as when you
wrote "Walt and Will" (originally titled "Disneyad")?

MA: We're talking editorial decisions. In my mind this was
a book I started which used to be called *The Disneyad*,
but it was published as *The Propheteers*. It's a product of
nine years' work—not consecutive, since I left it for
many years—but "Walt and Will" is part of the novel.
"The Oranging of America" was a story which I continued. I didn't see "Walt and Will" as a separate story.
My editor did, and he encouraged me to use that in *Free
Agents*. I thought I didn't want to use it because, to me, it

was part of the novel. It was his feeling that it wouldn't make any difference. Your question suggests to me my own feeling that it probably does: Why would anyone want to read it again? So I had to find a place for "Walt and Will" because that was a crucial part of the novel. To have that follow right after "The Oranging of America," which for me would have been two (previously published) pieces in a row, was not the way I wanted it. So I found a spot for "Walt and Will," but there again it occurred to me not to use it. Both those sections were too important so I had to trust that, statically being kind of old stuff, it wouldn't upset the flow of the novel.

I was trying to write a novel, and I want to say this because I think a lot of reviews have not gotten this, that if I could have kept my original title, *The Disneyad*, which the lawyers didn't let me keep, then maybe it would have been apparent. I was trying to write a mock epic. Behind *The Disneyad* was *The Iliad* and *The Aeniad*, and another mock epic, *The Dunciad*, which was so important to me. Just as every reader or listener of Homer knew that there was a Troy that had fallen, and knew all Priam's sons, so I'm counting on my readers to be familiar with Walt Disney and Disney World in Orlando. Of course, there's a big difference between Troy and Disney World—that's part of what the novel is about, part of its Kafkaesque and modernist comedy.

AV: Since you couldn't use the title *The Disneyad*, did you consider variations on the original title and how did you coin a new word with the title *The Propheteers*?

MA: A lawyer for Harper & Row insisted on the change (not using *The Disneyad*), and I'm sure he was correct. The content of a book is protected by the first amendment, you can use the name Walt Disney in the text, but the book jacket and title are considered advertising. So using the name Disney might be construed as infringement of what the Disney people own.

I couldn't think of any other title since I was so wedded to *The Disneyad*. I was in Buenos Aires at the time when I got the call that I needed a new title. My children and I walked the streets, but we couldn't think of one. Ted Solotaroff, my editor, came up with the new title. I'm very satisfied with it, but all those years I had the book in mind, it was *The Disneyad* to me and always will be.

AV: Most of the relationships your characters have seem fanciful. For example, Margery Post meets James Merriweather and quickly marries him. Then she meets Clarence Birdseye and runs off with him after a chance meeting in the Russian countryside. (Other fanciful relationships can be seen in such stories as "Vegetable Love" and "Carbo-Loading.") Why is your world so fanciful?

MA: That's not fanciful. It's called reality, biology, or other things. These are things that happen on the whole to everyone. I'm not much interested in describing a conventional courtship. I like the short cuts. It's not the fanciful I'm looking for in daily life to squeeze everything together.

For example, I wanted to set it up that Margery Post probably would have fallen in love with just about anybody. She has this guy with black teeth making passes at her in the middle of an absolute wilderness. She has a husband who is more interested in his gout and his black maids than he could ever be in her. She has a father who was interested in the next world and not this world. So this guy freezing berries puts one in her mouth and says she is the second person to taste berries over a year old. I think he said "it was as stiff as a hard-on." When you hear a line like that from a strange guy in the middle of nowhere, it doesn't seem to me that it's unlikely at all they would make love. It is just about inevitable. I think that's the way it is in the world.

AV: It seems you're fond of fanciful ways of saying something abstract.

MA: Fanciful isn't the word. Maybe the word is epiphany, but I don't see it as quite that either. I read an interview with García Márquez a few years ago, and someone asked him a similar question. I'm not comparing myself to García Márquez, but he said that he needed to render reality through surreal images in order to be faithful to its eerie strangeness. In one particular episode every time the woman touches a glass the glass turns blue. That was the way he found for saying "falling in love," for defamiliarizing it, as the critics say.

In my short story "Vegetable Love," the man and the waitress put on their running shoes and go off to Mexico. It means that his quest is for nothing less extravagant than the meaning of life. But if I put it like that, who would want to read it? Who would want to write it?

So I find a dramatic or metaphorical way of talking about, I hope, things that matter most to people. Poets get away with these tropes all the time. Really, twentieth-century fictions owe a lot to the narrative stock-in-trade poets and makers of fairy tales and folklore.

AV: Walt Disney's character is ironic since he makes everyone happy, but he is quite often depressed. Was this intentionally done?

MA: Very much. I have no idea what Walt was really like. If Walt Disney was really like that, his whole family and the world have my sympathy. I'm sure he wasn't. That's exactly the way I wanted him to be. I wanted him to be in great despair.

AV: Is C.W. Post, who is cast as a Nazirite, a metaphor for religion which many people now see as old-fashioned?

MA: I think it's been old-fashioned since Samson's time. But there are still Philistines.

AV: Margery Post and Bones Jones both come to realize their unhappiness with life is because they don't have kids and consequently don't understand children.

MA: I think you're reading a lot of my feelings about the

world and that I've lived very close to my children these last few years, especially. To me, that pretty much wraps up as to what the essence of life is. So if I have characters who seem arid and who think they have missed the world, then I guess they have if they haven't had children.

AV: The use of popular culture in contemporary fiction is a fascinating subject. Your novel contains some household words as characters: Howard Johnson, Walt Disney, Clarence Birdseye, C. W. Post, and Margery Post Merriweather. Why did you select these historical figures, and did you research their lives for accuracy?

MA: No, I didn't research them. I didn't even know Margery Post had met Birdseye. I like the names. I always liked the name Birdseye, and that little trademark has been in my mind since I was a kid. The disclaimer at the beginning of the novel, where I said that I was mostly acquainted with these people from my breakfast table, is the truth. I grew up in Grand Rapids, which is down the road from Battle Creek, and one of the earliest trips I took was to a cereal factory. People like the Posts and Kelloggs have been in my mind since childhood. Obviously, they are recognizable symbols of American success, and for that reason I can use them, as names or ciphers, not as realistic historical figures. I wanted to suggest that what motivates people who become household words is something more complicated than money.

If I called them John Smith or Allan Vorda or Max Apple, I would have to treat them more realistically, perhaps write about them as people who do want to earn more money. I don't believe anybody does anything for money. I know that sounds perfectly crazy. I mean everyday people, men and women who go to work in the morning to a store or factory, work for money. But someone who has ninety motels: Why do they want ninety-one or ninety-two or ninety-three? Or if someone has Disneyland: Why do they want Disney World? I'm just trying to imagine what it would be like because I think all of us know why we work. We work for a paycheck every week or every two weeks, but if I had one hundred million dollars I'd still work. You'd still work. Why does a writer with three books want another one?

It's the same thing. Why does someone who's drawn a series of cartoons want to draw another one? What's the blank page or open celluloid? Those are life and death questions. I can't just state them boldly, theologically, or religiously. There's no way to do it. The novel becomes a vision of what life is. Now maybe I've romanticized it, sentimentalized it. Maybe these moguls are awful people. No doubt some of them are. I read the paper, too; and, unfortunately, I've met some of them.

I was looking for a vision that is generous. I honestly believed from the few things I knew about Post or Kellogg that they still held an idea of making money for the sake of stewardship. C.W. Post believed very seriously that the world would be better if animals weren't killed. For me, this makes C.W. Post a much more interesting character. So he's not a case study in how to get rich or what money is. That is what most popular fiction, what little I've read, is about—rich people and how they got rich. You know, the page-turning best sellers by people like Judith Krantz.

I wanted to write another version of this fundamental American story. I was interested in the concept of money, but in a different way. I was interested in why C.W. Post didn't want his money. Why money doesn't mean any-thing to him or to Howard Johnson or, finally, Walt Disney. When I was creating Walt Disney I was trying to make a portrait of the artist. I think Disney was a great artist. You know Whitman's remark that "money is a form of poetry?" What if getting rich is not the sordid thing it's depicted to be in so many American novels? Or say that wealth might serve a writer now as Priam's wealth served Homer, as an opportunity to investigate the whole national character, its sweetness, its pathos, and its existential terrors. Maybe that's what more formula writers ought to be doing in their novels? I'm just asking.

AV: Or one might be rich and inherit it like Margery Post, yet even she's not totally happy.

MA: No, she's not. My sympathies with her are very great because this is a woman who has had virtually everything, but she has never been loved nor been able to. One of the saddest episodes in the book is when she's talking to the lawyer about when she goes through Orlando looking at children. She describes children climbing trees, and the lawyer says to her, "They're playing." This is what's missing because she doesn't know what playing is. She might be the richest woman in the world with mansions and all sorts of sophistication, but she doesn't know what play is and play is at the heart of life.

AV: Is Katherine Woodson, a minor figure who makes a late appearance in the novel, modeled after anyone?

MA: No.

AV: What was the reason for her appearance?

MA: I wanted Margery to be jealous of someone. Katherine Woodson is a woman who is beautiful and young. She's doing things, and Margery hates her. It's just realism, because here is a woman who has basically taken over her house and Margery doesn't like anyone very much.

AV: What prompted that whole sequence of bizarre, almost hallucinogenic, scenes with Walt Disney: cat-got-his-tongue in mental animation, the nurse moving her eyeballs, and the needle as Mr. Shovel?

MA: To me that's the core of the novel. I can't explain it, but that's the absolute center.

AV: The ending of *The Propheteers* is somewhat demonic where Walt is mildly electrocuting the Disney children who wait to return for more electrical shock treatment.

"As awful as it looked," you write, "as awful as it was, he was giving them what they wanted." Can you elaborate on this unconventional ending?

MA: I think the quote says all I can say. I wanted the end to be both a surprise and inevitable. That is, here we have the world as it is. I've shown in the novel that Walt Disney, who's depressed and brooding on death, is an artist who can't help but wonder what happens when he erases a line, thereby raising existential and metaphysical issues. He is not a happy man. So we wonder: What is the magic of Walt Disney? Like any artist, he works in loneliness. He works in that dreamy, dark undercurrent that produces both great joy and inexplicable despair. Margery Post, by contrast, works in a straightforward way. Money can do this; power can do this. I'll hire the lawyers. She understands the world, she thinks. So when there is a confrontation, I wanted it to be a confrontation between the artist and the world.

AV: It also deals with your other theme: art versus life.

MA: Yes. I can't make it any more bold than that. What I'm saying is the end is exactly what I wanted: to see, not only the triumph of Disney, but it's a comment about where art comes from. That this dreamy, depressed, hardly being able to get along in the world person can and does rise to do what nobody else can do. It may be somewhat awful, yet it's exactly what the world wants and deserves.

AV: I really thought that made it.

MA: I didn't know that I had it. I kept writing. I finished it, but I didn't have the end that I wanted. So I kept writing even after I sent it in because I had to get the ending just right.

AV: Another theme or motif I would like to review is the use of fruits and/or color. The first one that comes to mind, other than the apple which you never seem to make an issue, is the color orange associated with Howard Johnson in your story "The Oranging of America."

There is also the metaphor utilizing the orange-topped cryonic U-Haul freezer attached to his car for his secretary, Milly. What caused this inspiration?

MA: I don't know. That's all unconscious. The apple stuff doesn't mean anything to me other than you have to take your name into account. When I titled that story "The Oranging of America," it never occurred to me that it would come to readers as *The Oranging of America* by Max Apple. The punning and color stuff were absolutely lost on me until it was pointed out. It's just unconscious. I have no answer for that.

AV: There is also the extended metaphor of pomegranates in *The Propheteers*, supposedly painted by Dali for C.W. Post, being depicted on canvas as if they were people: round, hard, mysterious, pitted, tender, thick-skinned— above all, useless. Essentially, isn't C.W Post more like a pomegranate than a cornflake, just as Birdseye was more kale than orange juice?

MA: Yes. You're right. Nicely said. The honest answer that comes to mind is because I am acquainted with the Bible. I spent a lot of years at Hebrew school.

AV: Other than the fact the French word *pomme* means apple, why pomegranate?

MA: I *wondered* about pomegranates. When you're a kid, it's hard enough reading Hebrew and then you think: Why are pomegranates all over? Why a land of milk and honey? Milk and honey were things that weren't particularly interesting to me, either. I probably would have preferred Rice Krispies and milk. I never thought about this before, but I always wanted to eat cereal in the morning. For some reason my grandmother insisted that I drink coffee. My deepest longing, if you wonder why I write about cereal or why I have Dali talking about cornflakes moving, was to eat cereal. Also, I think I recaptured my childhood longing. I didn't want to sit in the house and have hard toast and coffee with my grandmother and watch my grandfather drink tea with a piece of sugar in his mouth. I was sitting with my immigrant grandparents having breakfast and imagining that they were in Odessa and I wanted to be in Grand Rapids and Battle Creek. So I think that explains some of it, too, but pomegranates are a kind of odd, unusual fruit. Even now when you see them in the supermarket, it seems like more work than they are worth. I guess I could have picked artichokes, but the Bible is not littered with artichokes. You are right, I did describe it as people.

AV: It's interesting to go back to Shakespeare's sonnets which state there are two types of immortality: procreation and creation. *The Propheteers* seems to suggest the artist has a certain type of immortality with his creative work. On the other hand, so-called famous people, like C.W. Post at the end of the novel, are forgotten. They become a generic company like General Foods with their real names lost in time.

MA: Even Shakespeare will disappear. I would also say that people who do create don't understand what life is all about. Believe me, I don't pose to know what life is all about. Writing for me is *a continuing act of wonder*. I make small discoveries along the way. I get the felicity of a line now and then such as at the end of this novel, or the passage about Disney, or the chapter about the tongue. When I get something—I don't always get it, believe me, the way I want it—that's what I'm struggling for. When I get parts of the story or novel, that's pure bliss, pure felicity, and that's as close to understanding the world as I can get. Maybe a craftsman gets it in another way, such as when the feel of the wood is just right. I'm sure it's available to other people when you feel things are just right and great. Every once in a while, the world seems luminous: being in love or with your children.

The other thing we carry with us is our death. Maybe I'm obsessed with those things, and it's possible I am. I've told you about the relations with my grandparents and how I grew up living close to old people. One of my earliest jobs—I recently wrote a short essay about this—was taking care of my grandpa, not that he needed any care. He was a vivid and active man who lived to be one hundred and seven years old, but he was an old man when I was born. He was over sixty-five. So, in that sense, I lived close to death. One of my big fears was that my grandpa would die, even though he was more vivid and alive than people much younger, because he was working eighteen hours a day. So that's why I think death is with me, because I've lived so close to it.

AV: Disney makes the analogy on pages 166–67 that the artist is like God drawing lines (life) and then erasing them (death). This recalls Ebeneezer Cooke's existentialist notions of killing the ant in Barth's *The Sot-Weed Factor*.

MA: I wonder about the erased lines. What happens to a line that is erased? What happens when there is a page that's covered with things that disappear? What happens to people when they die? These are things that people have always wondered about. They go one way into religion, which becomes solidified. I'm not a theologian and I don't pretend to be, but all people wonder about what life is and what death is.

I don't remember if there is any connection with *The Sot-Weed Factor*. It might have stayed in my own unconscious because *The Sot-Weed Factor* is one of the greatest novels I've ever read. So I wouldn't be surprised. I would like to say any borrowings I got from *The Sot-Weed Factor* or Barth can only enrich one's work.

AV: In chapter nineteen, Nurse Bloom is unable to get any blood from Disney. Essentially, he is like an animated character, isn't he?

MA: Exactly. I wanted him to be as depressed, as lifeless, as full of death, as I possibly could. It's the blank page idea again. The novel in part is about how the imagination creates words, people, out of nothing, as God did the world. So for all that I've made an anatomy of melancholy in Disney's character, I've also made the kind of affirmative statement, I hope, that I described earlier. It's a comic novel. Like the Disney children, we're all attracted to humor and humorous people because we sense the sorrow and pain behind the humor, and that's real life.

AV: With the deaths of Camus and Sartre it seems existentialism has died. I can't think of one major writer who has said, "God is dead." What was once a major movement now seems dormant. Why?

MA: I have no way to answer that except that it isn't. Writers don't have to make such statements because it is so obvious. I hardly even know in any academic sense what existentialism is, except in my own life. I think it is so much the mood and the understanding of the world, since there are people who read and think, that it doesn't have to be stated any more.

So that's why everybody is so busy being something else, Born Again or whatever, because you've gotten beat over the head about something that isn't there. The reality is existentialism. How you live with it is another matter.

AV: What are your feelings about contemporary fiction? Do you feel comfortable with labels like metafiction or experimental fiction, which are sometimes applied to your work?

MA: The truth is I don't like to categorize. I'm as likely to enjoy fiction that is old-fashioned as something avant-garde. My current colleague Lynne Sharon Schwartz's novel *Disturbances in the Field* is perfectly realistic, conventional narrative and could have been written, stylistically speaking, in the nineteenth century. It's wonderful. It is one of the great novels in the way that George Eliot's

and Joseph Conrad's are great—intricate plot, richly realized characters, acute social commentary. So I can appreciate that. I can also appreciate Frederick Barthelme
or Raymond Carver and other writers who shade away
from the mainstream. I consider what I do as sometimes
experimental, sometimes very conventional.

AV: Or post-modernist?

MA: I was invited to write "Post-Modernism" (reprinted in
Free Agents) for a panel discussion at a museum. First, I
went to a library to find out what post-modernism was. I
ended up reading a book of literary criticism that used
my work as an example. So I thought, if I'm part of it I
ought to be able to describe it. But, of course, it's critics
who make the categories. That's what I was playing with
in the "Post-Modernism" piece: writers don't say, "Today I'm a realist," or "Now I'm going to write a minimalist story." We write what we can, including the bad writers. I think Louis L'Amour might have his existentialist
days and Judith Krantz now and then feels minimalist.
You hope that the critics won't stick you with a label—
Georgian poet, Decadent novelist—that will diminish
you. You hope that, like Dickens or Joyce, your work will
defy any one label and accommodate all of them.

The real question is, when will I have time to read all
the contemporary fiction I want? I think there are an
enormous number of good writers in the country today. I
think this is a golden age in fiction writing. I know the
critics, those people who are taking the measure and who
have their hand on the pulse of the times, are never going
to get it. You have to wait another generation or two for
it. So people are upset that there is no Faulkner they can
pick out. Of course, in Faulkner's lifetime, until almost
the end, no one picked him out either.

AV: Would you be willing to name writers you admire? Or
those who have influenced you?

MA: There are so many that I would just as soon not

answer. As soon as you mention Barth, certainly. He's brought so much joy to my life, especially when I was young. Now I read my contemporaries with admiration and respect. I know a lot of them now, too. That's why I'd feel bad if I'd start giving a list and I'd leave out some.

I can tell you that when I was young, and by that I mean eighteen or so, it was a great discovery for me to find the Jewish writers. Not only Bellow and Malamud, but Herbert Gold. A whole group of writers who seemed so different from me, though their idioms and characters were intimately familiar.

I knew as a teenager that I was going to be a writer, whatever that meant. I was living close to stories. My grandmother was a great storyteller. And I knew that being a writer meant being a reader, too. Reading was the most important thing in the world to me. When I was sixteen or seventeen, I read everything I could get my hands on. I didn't know when I read Dostoyevsky that I was reading a translation. I just read any book I could find, and given my later practice, I was strangely attracted to immense and realistic novels like *Les Miserables*. I made the jump, literally, from juvenile fiction to that book; I couldn't stop reading it. It turned out that I was reading great fiction, though I didn't know it at the time.

I thought that real writers were not people like me. I thought they were Englishmen or Frenchmen or Russians. I thought you had to be full of high seriousness like T.S. Eliot. Then when I got to college and got a closer look at all that high seriousness and great tradition, I knew I didn't belong to any of that. When you realize that you're not going to be writing about the Russian aristocracy or the French bourgeoisie, you look around for models closer to home, and this is where Malamud and Gold, especially, were so helpful.

I feel enormously close to E. L. Doctorow's writing,

too—both to the life he recounts, the autobiographical stuff, and to his style as a fiction writer. I also love Grace Paley's stories. Some of these stories just sing to me. Once I was teaching a short summer session at Berkeley with Grace Paley and E. L. Doctorow. Students would go from one class to another. One of the stories reminded me of a certain Chekhov story which I made an allusion to. A student stood up and said, "This has got to be a fix! I was in Doctorow's class and Grace Paley's class and they were both talking about the same Chekhov story!" Of course, we had not mentioned it between us, but it shows our affinity as readers and writers.

AV: Your review titled "Merdistes in Fiction's Garden" lambasted John Gardner's *On Moral Fiction*. It seems Gardner accomplished three things: (1) he made a lot of writers and critics mad; (2) he escalated critical attention on John Fowles by making him out to be the greatest writer of this century; and (3) Gardner may be remembered more for *On Moral Fiction* than *October Light* or *Sunlight Dialogues*. Do you have any comments ten years after your review of his book?

MA: I would stay with what I said, except that I later met Gardner and I found him to be charming. A very nice man. I liked him a lot. He had no animosity about the review. I took him seriously, by the way, because I spent a lot of time on that review. He was just wrong, and, you know what, he knew it. I think he wanted to make large statements. When you try to do something on a large scale, you're going to fall most of the time. So I gave him credit for what he tried to do. Of course, in a way, he was right; but in all the specifics he was wrong. I found it very objectionable to bring in Homer to pommel Ron Sukenick. It was disproportionate. So I brought out Homer to pommel him.

AV: Your stories are often set in Michigan, where you were raised and educated, or in Texas, where you teach at Rice

University. Do you choose these settings because they have had an impact upon you, or is it just their familiarity?

MA: Not consciously. Things happen to you in a place in the world. I know names of streets in Grand Rapids and Houston. I don't know them in Paris. Some of *The Propheteers* takes place in Italy when Margery goes to look at *The Last Supper*. A friend gave me a guide book to Italy so I could look up some street names. What I do know are the places where I've lived, but places are not important to me. I used to talk to Bill Goyen, who is a friend and a great writer from Texas. He didn't live in Houston because that was his place and he had to go away from it. He is so much rooted in place. His fiction is the place. To me, it's the opposite. My characters, I think, could just about live anywhere, but I don't know the street names.

AV: *The Oranging of America* was one of the most distinctive collections of short stories to appear in recent decades. I think it stands right up there with Borges' *Labyrinths* and Barth's *Lost in the Funhouse*. How did these stories develop?

MA: I knew when I was ready. I sent "The Oranging of America" to Ted Solotaroff at *American Review*, and after he published it, other stories came rapidly. When I started to be published I realized I had some readers. I wasn't alone, as I had been all those years in graduate school, writing my secret stuff in the back of my Shakespeare and Milton notebooks, almost as if it were Hebrew starting from the other side of the page. None of these stories was published—typical juvenilia set down in my mid-twenties without any real hope.

I felt I was going to be a writer someday, and I thought I was going to be a teacher, but I knew I was never going to be a literary critic. Writing a dissertation was a pose for me, but I wrote it on a text that was intriguing: *The Anatomy of Melancholy*, a seventeenth-century book that addresses subjects I take up in *The Propheteers*. The career I have now is the one I still want. I still teach. I spend some hours almost every day being a writer, but I spend more hours being a reader. If you ask me what I am, I'm a reader.

AV: Regarding your narrative style, you have said in an interview with the *Mississippi Review* (Fall 1984) that "Gas Stations" was a crucial story for you "because it was the first time I consciously trusted my fantastic impulses completely." Can you elaborate on this statement? Does this following of fantastic impulses apply only to the short story?

MA: I hope so. I don't want to follow too many fantastic impulses in the world, though I have them. About "Gas Stations," Nora Ephron had called me from *Esquire* and said she liked my work and wanted to know if I'd write something for their bicentennial issue. She started running through a list of possible topics, which always strikes dread in my heart. I had never had anything published in any large-circulation magazines. So I said I would write on gas stations, my suggestion. And yet I began to follow her advice in writing the essay; it was more than advice, it was directions. There was a lot of money at stake, and I nervously produced a rather dull essay on gas stations, which I threw away. Then I wrote what I wanted. I remember this so distinctly because I sent it to her with trepidation—with real fear that I'd blown my big chance for money and fame.

I was on vacation when Nora tracked me down and told me how much she loved the piece. I said, "But it's not an essay." She said, "Who cares! When it's that good, who cares!" That gave me a lot of confidence just at the time I needed to trust my own instincts and personal style. Maybe that dull essay would have been published anyway, but I wouldn't have *emerged* as a writer, following my own directions.

AV: The last line of "Gas Stations" reads: "Careful on the curves, amid kisses and hopes I gave her the gas." This autoerotic metaphor recalls e.e. cummings' poem "she being brand new." Was this a conscious attempt to imitate cummings?

MA: Not conscious, but you picked up something good. No, I didn't know it. I just do it. I remember working those lines carefully. I do it all by rhythms to get it just right.

AV: What was the inspiration for "Vegetable Love?" Also discuss Annette's concept of Ferguson's fidelity depending more upon abstaining from meat than from other women.

MA: I haven't read it in so many years that I really couldn't answer that. But my wife and I had a small health food store, right down the street here on Morningside, and on the porch we used to be referred to as the Gypsy Market.

AV: What was the store called?

MA: Apples, Arts, & Herbs. It was a really tiny place. We sold toys on consignment. It was closed down by the health department because Jessica, our daughter, was playing with lima beans on the floor. No one ever bought any dried lima beans. We had about forty pounds of them, but the health inspector said you couldn't have children playing with food and then sell it. I suppose the eating that I've talked about was on my mind when I wrote "Vegetable Love."

AV: What prompted an ivory tower Ph.D. to write his first novel, *Zip*, about a poor Jewish manager of a Puerto Rican middleweight fighter? Also, what problems did this present as far as your authorial voice in connection with the novel being related in an unusual semi-foreshadowing style?

MA: I just don't remember. A writer has to forget, like anyone else; otherwise, I would still be writing *Zip*. I'm busy forgetting *The Propheteers*.

AV: At the end of *Zip*, J. Edgar Hoover sits in a balloon above the ring. Any connection to similar scenes in Waugh's *Vile Bodies* or Barth's *Giles Goat-Boy*?

MA: I haven't read Waugh's *Vile Bodies*, but I did read *Giles Goat-Boy*. I tell you what it is. Writers that live at the same time, given all our differences, we're like radios since we're playing back certain images. The language is finite.

AV: "Bridging" (from *Free Agents*) is an incredibly poignant story made even more so because it is difficult to separate the fiction from the reality of your own life: a widowed father raising two children. You also stated in your interview with the *Mississippi Review* that your father's death affected you "in all sorts of ways that must filter into my fiction," but that you also lost "that intense ambition to be a writer." How has the death of two people so very close to you affected your writing and your view of life?

MA: I can't answer that any other way except that it shows up in the work. I just can't answer any more than that. Except that it is there.

AV: The two-pronged sword of writing and teaching beleaguers most writers with not enough time for both. What are your thoughts on this, since you have vacillated between writing short stories and novels as well as screenplays?

MA: I don't get ideas. The screenplays or the things that are commissioned I only do if it is offered. I don't sit around and dream up screenplays. I've learned something about writing screenplays. It's not a form that's a happy one for a writer because in the final version the words aren't everything. I like to be close to words.

With the fiction sometimes I'm interested in all the forms. When I start I'm with a blank page. I don't know that a story is ever going to be a story. I can feel about halfway through. I start to know. I feel it is going to be a story and not a novel, but some things are just going to be novels. It's happened a couple of times. Talking about an existential situation, I don't know what I'm writing. The majority turns out to be nothing—neither novels nor stories—just an interesting passage here and there. They turn out to be fragments. So I just have to trust my judgment.

AV: Finally, in what direction do you see your fiction going?

MA: In an article I published this year in the *New York Times Book Review* I talked about finding my place on the dying body of fiction. This goes back to Henry James' phrase, about the novel being the body of American fiction. I said, "Finally, I found a place. It was under the left middle fingernail, an aging subdivision called 'Jewish, Jewish-American, not so Jewish and not so American either.' It was one of the noisiest sectors on the body, but I slipped in and found a place that had been vacated when the inhabitant moved to Hollywood. As crowded and argumentative as the subdivision was, I was relieved to have finally found my own place."

In the act of writing a novel or story, I'm dreaming. I'm daydreaming. It's the most real, the most profound *me* there can be, which doesn't mean it's very real or very profound. I was learning, even before I went to the University of Michigan, how to tell a story and also what to leave out. I don't consider myself a master of this. I give myself assignments. They come from my unconscious and, when the raw materials are there, I work with it as well as I can. I'm still learning. I hope to learn to do this better and better. That's the work of my life. My writings are my motels. My hope is to have a chain.

A Fish Swims in My Lung

AN INTERVIEW WITH

Cristina Garcia

CRISTINA GARCIA was born on July 4, 1958, in Havana, Cuba. She was only two years old when her family decided to leave Cuba for the United States after Castro came to power, and she grew up in New York City, where she attended Barnard College. Later, she attended the Johns Hopkins University School of Advanced International Studies and then worked as a correspondent for *Time* magazine in Miami, San Francisco, and Los Angeles. She is currently a visiting professor at Princeton University.

Her first novel, *Dreaming in Cuban*, was nominated for the National Book Award in 1992. She, her husband, Scott Brown, and baby daughter, Pilarita, live in Princeton, New Jersey.

The interview was conducted by phone on January 23, 1993. Ms. Garcia spoke from her home in Princeton, the only break occurring when she had to pause to feed her daughter.

AV: You were born in Havana, Cuba, in 1958, and moved to the United States when you were only two years old. What effect did this have on you and your family?

CG: We moved to New York and had a different experience growing up than the larger exile community which moved to Miami. I think we were just like any other immigrant family that comes to New York or any other big city. We grew up bilingual, and my parents worked very hard. I was so young when I left that I had no memories of Cuba, and my parents were so busy working they weren't necessarily nostalgic the way many other Cuban families are. It had no direct effect on me because I was simply in the wake of this dislocation of my parents. I grew up very Americanized and was much too young to remember the trauma of moving. For me, a larger effect was that my family was split up. All of my mother's side of the family stayed in Cuba—by choice—and all my father's family came here. I grew up with that political schism as the backdrop of my family life.

AV: What was it like growing up in New York during the 1970s, and what was your educational background like?

CG: I was educated in Catholic schools through high school. I received a degree in political science from Barnard College, and then I went to Johns Hopkins University, where I received a master's degree in international relations.

Growing up in New York was great. I grew up partly in Queens, the other part in Brooklyn Heights, and then I went to high school and college in Manhattan. I've always felt like a New Yorker through and through.

AV: Where you lived in New York, was that part of a Cuban neighborhood?

CG: No, not at all. I lived in Brooklyn Heights, which is right across the river from Wall Street. It's just a corner of Brooklyn, and it's quite an upscale neighborhood.

AV: Which writers influenced you? Your style seems to have elements of García Márquez and Borges. I was also wondering if John Barth influenced you, since you attended Johns Hopkins.

CG: I did attend Johns Hopkins, but since I went to their advanced international studies program I had nothing to do with their English department or their graduate writing program. I've read Barth, but I couldn't consider him influential in my writing. I have read and loved all the great Latin American authors, including García Márquez and Borges, whom you mentioned, but also Jorge Amado from Brazil and Julio Cortázar from Argentina. I also loved great poets such as Octavio Paz, Pablo Neruda, and Federico García Lorca. Strangely enough, I came to them rather late, as I was in my twenties. When I was growing up, I read most of the great Russian, French, and American writers before encountering any Spanish or Latin writers.

Among contemporary writers, I love Toni Morrison and Louise Erdrich, who writes about Native American life in the Dakotas. I'll tell you who I had on my desk when I was writing *Dreaming in Cuban*. I had a copy of poems by Wallace Stevens, García Márquez's *One Hundred Years of Solitude*, and Morrison's *Song of Solomon*.

AV: Did your background as a *Time* correspondent assist you in becoming a writer?

CG: It's totally different. In fact, fiction, for me, is kind of anti-journalism since it uses a different portion of my brain. The only way journalism was helpful to me was the sheer physical comfort I had when sitting in front of a computer for hours at a time. It was more of a physiognomic advantage.

AV: You left Cuba in 1961 and returned to visit your family in 1984. You said your trip to Cuba "was like finding the missing link in my own identity." For five years you couldn't get the trip out of your mind, whereupon you wrote *Dreaming in Cuban*, which reveals how strong memory can be. To what extent was the writing of *Dreaming in Cuban* a cathartic experience?

CG: I have no memories of Cuba prior to going back in 1984. The only memories I have of Cuba are the two weeks I spent there in 1984 whereupon I learned a lot of my family history. It definitely enlarged my perspective on the choices family members made, particularly those who chose to remain in Cuba. Furthermore, it enlarged my sense of self and my own identity and how Cuban I was—which I never realized until then.

AV: Was it hard to get into Cuba?

CG: In those days, before Radio Martí started up in south Florida, it was not that difficult. They had charter flights leaving Miami on a fairly regular basis. It was quite expensive, and that was prohibitive. And there were waiting lists, but it was not impossible to go at that point. Since then it has been very difficult.

AV: Do you see writers such as Sandra Cisneros, Oscar Hijuelos, Julia Alvarez, Victor Villaseñor, and yourself as being hybrids of such Latin American writers as Borges, García Márquez, and Vargas Llosa? Or are the American-born and/or raised Hispanic writers offering a different perspective of their ethnicity than their South American counterparts?

CG: I think probably the latter. I think the experiences are so different, and yet I'm sure we all draw on our reading and from such writers as Borges and García Márquez. It's part of our literary heritage, and I think, for those of us who grew up in the U.S., we are talking about a different experience entirely. I also think we're not so much on the periphery. I think what's happening in what was once considered mainstream "America" is changing, and I think American literature is reflecting that.

AV: In Earl Shorris' book *Latinos: A Biography of the People*, which chronicles the past and present influences of Latinos in the United States, he writes, "There are no Latinos, only diverse peoples struggling to remain who they are while becoming someone else." Do you agree with this statement regarding Cuban-Americans? And doesn't this statement also work conversely as sundry new ethnic groups exert their influence upon Americans who lose a little of their own heritage as part of the proverbial melting pot?

CG: I think so. I think the idea of a melting pot is an arcane one. I think what happens is that by the third generation most immigrants would not be speaking their parent's native tongue or their grandparent's native tongue. I think there's an emphasis now and a value placed on the diversity of speaking more than one language in a way that didn't exist before. For example, I hope my daughter, Pilarita, will grow up and speak Spanish because I'm going to speak Spanish to her. My husband is half Japanese, and I will encourage his mother to speak Japanese to my daughter in order to continue the heritage. There's an emphasis and a value placed on the continuation of heritage whereas before assimilation was the key to success. Now the broader your background and the more languages you speak, the more advantageous it is in society.

AV: When Felicia is six she brings home a mother-of-pearl shell that Celia says will "bring bad luck." Shortly thereafter a tidal wave hits. It seems bad luck, especially concerning her romantic relationships, follows Felicia everywhere. Even her use of santería with its black magic doesn't help. Why is Felicia cursed? Is it because she is the only offspring of Celia to remain in Cuba?

CG: I don't think it's any one reason why Felicia is cursed. It's a panoply of factors that have worked against her in her life. Felicia was a daughter born in an unhappy marriage, a daughter who never got the approval of her father the same way her elder sister did, a daughter who didn't have the same kind of resolve or talent that her older sister did, and a daughter who was always searching for something. After the revolution she didn't find it in politics or in volunteerism. So in a quest to find some satisfaction in her life, I think she was drawn to santería through her friends and into love affairs. I think that was her way of giving meaning to her life. I don't think there was just one thing. I can't really agree that she is cursed. I think that is the way her life turned out, but I certainly didn't plan it that way.

AV: Did you have to do any research and did your family provide any information when you were working on the santería scenes?

CG: My family provided no information on the santería. It was not something I grew up with. It was something the character Felicia led me to and then I had to scramble and research to keep up with the forays into santería.

AV: Why did you switch from a third-person to a first-person narrative with the appearance of Pilar Puente? Don't you think some readers will assume Pilar is a persona for the author?

CG: I think a lot of people have erroneously assumed that. I tried to write her in the third person, but her first-person voice kept punching through the third person. I guess it was appropriate for her in the way she spoke and her vernacular that she have her own voice in a way the others didn't. I would also like to point out that Celia has a first-person voice through her letters. Even though it is a more formal outlet, we do get a sense of her and how she thinks through the first-person narrative in her letters.

AV: There is an interesting thought that Pilar has: "My father knew I understood more than I could say." Can you comment on Pilar's thoughts, since this expresses a basic challenge for writers—to articulate their innermost thoughts?

CG: I think Pilar in the book was kind of blessed with special powers as a baby, which may be viewed as a type of magical realism. Pilar could make the nanny's hair fall out, she could will things to happen, and she could talk to her grandmother late at night in the dark. She was someone who had some connection with the supernatural, which she could control as a child. I think she lost this special power to some degree when she was in the U.S., but it came back to some degree when she discovered santería quite by accident. I think her father had a sense he had a very special baby, in that there was something luminous and intelligent about this child. When he spoke to her she knew more than what she could say at that point.

AV: What was the inspiration behind the beautiful sentence that Celia writes to Gustavo: "A fish swims in my lung?"

CG: That just came to me. When you have a heartbreak it describes what your chest feels like. It does feel like a fish swimming in your lung: that intense and fluttering and pressured uncertainty that one gets when one is heart-broken.

AV: There is the scene where Lourdes is raped by the Cuban soldier and she smells all the major events of his life. How did you create this scene? Also, why is Lourdes' vision of the rapist based on smelling while Felicia's gift of perception is based on the sense of hearing?

CG: That scene was a total surprise to me. I can remember very distinctly when I was writing it that it was summer in Los Angeles. I didn't plan for Lourdes to be raped or visualize it moving to that inevitability. It was just one of those moments, if you are lucky, that happens occasionally in fiction. It feels as if it's being not dictated to you but that a little part of the sky opens up to you and it flows down upon you. It wasn't planned. It was a gift.

AV: The rapist carves something illegible into Lourdes' stomach. What is this supposed to mean? Also, are the rape and carving scenes, which foreshadow her bloody miscarriage, symbolically connected to the sacrificial blood rites of the santería?

CG: No, I don't think they are connected to the santería. The way I wrote it was simply a vicious act by a deranged soldier. I think what happens is it leaves a scar she carries with her the rest of her life. It reminds her of that dreadful day and about her hatred of the Cuban system after the revolution.

AV: The color blue is used frequently throughout the novel,

often in the form of magical realism. Since García Márquez is considered one of the innovators of magical realism and has used the color blue as a device in his fiction, have you experienced any criticism for covering the same territory?

CG: Nobody has ever mentioned that, and I didn't have García Márquez in mind. What I had in mind with the color blue is the mental image one has of an island. Cuba is surrounded by water, and that is why there is so much blue in the book. Celia has a house on the beach, and so her entire horizon is blue. It colors her entire life and perspective.

AV: It's ironic that Lourdes rejects Cuba for the cold of New York City while her daughter wants to return to the warmth of Cuba. Does Lourdes unconsciously think the weather will freeze her bad memories (e.g., her rape by the Cuban soldiers) of Cuba?

CG: I think there was an element of that, because when she and her family arrived in Miami she insisted they drive north. I think she just wanted to get so cold, almost a numbing cold, that it would free her of her memories.

AV: Felicia thinks her mother has an unnatural attraction to El Líder—an attraction that is almost sexual—and then, later on, Felicia fantasizes about having sex with El Líder. Does Castro represent the missing man in each of their lives?

CG: I think Castro for many years was a powerful sex symbol in Cuba. He did sleep with many women in Cuba and has many children scattered around the island. I think he represented a kind of sexual fantasy for many women.

AV: Javier del Pino, Celia's son, is a professor of biochemistry in Czechoslovakia who lectures in Russian, German and Czech. Does the distancing between Javier and his daughter—who cannot speak fluent Spanish—show they are losing their Cuban heritage since they no longer speak the same language as their ancestors?

CG: I think so, in the fact that Javier loses his entire family and later his wife runs off with someone else. Javier returns to his homeland and becomes a broken man who has no family and no country of his own.

AV: What is your attitude toward Communism since certain elements in your novel seem to express a negative viewpoint?

CG: I grew up in a very black-and-white situation. My parents were virulently anti-Communist, and yet my relatives in Cuba were tremendous supporters of Communism, including members of my family who belong to the Communist Party. The trip in 1984 and the book, to some extent, were an act of reconciliation for the choices everybody made. I'm very much in favor of democratic systems, but I also strongly believe a country should determine its own fate. I realize I couldn't write and be a journalist and do everything I've done in Cuba; yet, I respect the right of people to live as they choose.

AV: What is the significance of Hugo making love to the prostitute with the black mask?

CG: There is no particular reason the prostitute wears the black mask. There is an earlier scene of Hugo with his wife having sex in the hotel, which shows he was interested in rougher or sadomasochistic rituals. I think that was his personal preference, but I don't think it has any larger significance. I think the significant thing wasn't the woman wearing the mask, but that his son Ivanito, whom he had never met, unfortunately saw Hugo for the first time under these conditions. It was a big disappointment and a shock to the boy.

AV: Lourdes decides "she has no patience for dreamers, for people who live between black and white." Do you consider Lourdes a tragic figure because she is more of a realist than a visionary like her mother and daughters?

CG: I wouldn't call Lourdes tragic, but I think she's a character with enormous blind spots. I think she is someone who lives and accomplishes things her way and, in that sense, considers herself a mover and a shaker and a success. I think this is how she measures other people. Perhaps Lourdes is tragic in the larger sense, but Lourdes would not consider herself a tragic figure.

AV: Felicia's unjustified attack on Graciela Moreira is sadistically bizarre as she applies a mixture of lye and menstrual blood when she gives Graciela a permanent. Why did you choose this action? Was it based on any particular incident?

CG: It wasn't based on any particular incident. I think Felicia was just mad. It made no sense, but she was deranged and upset after her second husband was killed. She became very paranoid—such as being distrustful of people with glasses. Graciela was just a victim of Felicia's deteriorating mental condition.

AV: After her attack on Graciela, Felicia is unaware of the passage of time. Can the same thing be said metaphorically about Cuba, which has been isolated from most of the world?

CG: I think Felicia has a bout of amnesia and drops out for a while, but I don't think a comparison should be made to Cuba. I think, for its size, Cuba has had an incredible influence and presence in the world. I don't think anybody has ever forgotten about Cuba. Even though it has been isolated, Cuba is constantly in the news. I believe it gets a disproportionate share of the world's interest.

AV: The role of the artist is a minor theme in the novel. Could you expand upon the differences of Pilar, who is an abstract painter in America, and Simón Córdoba, a fifteen-year-old Cuban boy, who is told by Celia to reorient his short stories toward the revolution? Have you ever wondered whether you might have been like Simón Córdoba and not had any creative freedom if your family had stayed in Cuba?

CG: I used that scene with Simón Córdoba only to illustrate the militancy and singlemindedness of Celia, especially when it came to her system and her way of life. It was written to illustrate one of Celia's blind spots and to see how people, if you keep them in dreams, are sacrificed by politics.

AV: It is ironic that Celia and Lourdes, who are estranged from each other by philosophy and distance, are alike in the sense that both are involved in the application of justice—Celia as a local judge and Lourdes as an auxiliary policeman. Why did you present the contrast where Celia presided as judge over a love affair contested by the postmaster's wife and by Lourdes, who indirectly caused the Navarro boy to jump into the river and drown?

CG: To answer the question of why there is such a contrast, it's because I was intrigued by the possibilities of interpretation when it came to patriotism. For Celia, patriotism in Cuba meant judging a variety of pieces from the sublime to the ridiculous. For Lourdes, patriotism in the United States was achieved through patrolling in order to maintain law and order. I would also like to say that I don't think Lourdes caused the Navarro boy, not even indirectly, to jump into the river and drown. I think he was planning to jump and she was trying to save him.

AV: Are there any similarities between the author and Pilar? For example, liking the music of Lou Reed, modeling nude at art school, being an atheist, or the belief that one has to live in the world to say anything meaningful about it.

CG: I have never modeled nude. My husband loves Lou Reed, which is how I started to love his music, but I didn't know anything about Lou Reed as a teenager. The whole punk element is not from personal experience, but this was also borrowed from my husband and I picked his brain a lot for that aspect of Pilar. I would say I identify with being an atheist and the belief that one has to live in the world to say anything meaningful about it.

AV: Jorge del Pino committed Celia to an asylum and then

to a house by the sea to make her forget her Spanish lover, but Celia's unmailed letters prove she hasn't forgotten. Aren't these unmailed letters similar to Celia's children and grandchildren who can't forget their memories and love of Cuba?

CG: I think for her it's simply a kind of diary; I think it's a private act of rebellion and optimism, in a strange way. That's what those letters are for Celia.

AV: Why didn't Celia mail the letters or try to go to Spain if she was so desperately in love with Gustavo?

CG: Celia did send him that first letter and never got a response. When she decided to marry Jorge del Pino I think Celia gave the public side of herself over to Jorge del Pino, but I think there was a private corner of herself that would always be for her lover. I think the cache of unmailed letters is illustrative of her private love for Gustavo.

AV: "Cuba is a peculiar exile, I think, an island colony. We can reach it by a thirty-minute charter flight from Miami, yet never reach it at all." The act of dreaming is a major motif that permits characters to take off on a mentally chartered flight whenever they have the notion. While Pilar's dreaming can be viewed as nostalgic, Celia's dreaming seems to have more in common with the madness of Felicia since she never mails her love letters to Gustavo. How do you view the different types of dreaming by Pilar and Celia?

CG: I think it's just extensions of their individual obsessions and concerns. When I was writing the book, I did not have any larger agenda nor was I parcelling out information to the characters. What I was doing was trying to stay as close as possible to their idiosyncrasies, obsessions, compulsions, and joys. The dreams they have stem simply from their individual traits.

AV: Pilar starts "dreaming in Spanish" after arriving in Cuba and wakes up "feeling different, like something inside me is changing, something chemical and irreversible." This scene shows Pilar regaining her Cuban heritage, but if this change is irreversible, why does she have to return to New York?

CG: I don't think it's irreversible in the literal sense, but I think it's irreversible in terms of her own identity since her "Cubanness" is now taking place.

AV: *Dreaming in Cuban* ends with Celia's death and her last letter to Gustavo. It doesn't matter whether one lives in America or Cuba since virtually the entire book seems to be full of lost loves, family estrangements, painful experiences, and various types of insanity. Is there any hope for your characters to be happy, to live with their loved ones and to have their dreams fulfilled?

CG: Probably not.

AV: What future do you see for Cuba, including her relationship with the United States?

CG: It looks pretty dismal right now. I think they have retrenched themselves into a terrible hole both financially and politically. There doesn't seem to be any flexibility in Cuba's policy. Similarly, I think the persistent isolationism and ostracism of the United States is unconscionable and should stop.

AV: Do you think this might change with the election of Bill Clinton, or perhaps with the death of Castro?

CG: I think it will be more likely with the death of Castro. I think Clinton has already indicated the U.S. policy will change very little toward Cuba.

AV: What were your thoughts when you heard you were nominated for the National Book Award?

CG: I don't know if it was coincidental, but I went into labor and had the baby the next day. After I gave birth, the next six weeks were like a baby blizzard until the National Book Awards. I was barely conscious at the ceremony, but I think it will sink in, in retrospect.

AV: Will your next book deal with your Cuban heritage, and what direction do you see yourself going as a writer?

CG: I do have a second novel in the works. The characters

are Cuban, but aside from that, there is no direct link
with the first novel. I prefer not to discuss it at this point
since it's in an early stage and things often change. For
example, the original title of my first novel was *Tropic of
Resemblances*.

AV: Since you have a political background, I wonder if your
   writing will function as political commentary.

CG: I think the nature of the exile is inherently political. I
   think there will always be politics just because that's a
   part of the fabric in the characters' lives, but it won't be
   political in the sense of agendas or axes to grind. It will be
   political to the extent that my characters are vastly interested in politics because I am an exile.

I Come from a Place That's Very Unreal

AN INTERVIEW WITH

Jamaica Kincaid

J AMAICA K INCAID was born into tropical poverty as Elaine Potter Richardson in 1949 on the island of Antigua. An only child, she lived with her father, a carpenter, and her mother in a house that had no electricity, water, or bathroom facilities. In "In the Night," she refers to a time in her youth when she would prepare the family outhouse every Wednesday for the night-soil men to pick up their tub and replace it with a clean one.

Since Antigua was a British colony, she was educated in the British system but grew to detest everything about England, except the literature. (Antigua became self-governing in 1967 and an independent nation within the Commonwealth in 1981.) After completing her secondary education at seventeen, she was sent to Westchester, New York, to work as an *au pair*. Later, she studied photography at the New School and attended Franconia College in New Hampshire.

In 1973 she changed her name to Jamaica Kincaid, and her writing caught the attention of William Shawn, editor of the *New Yorker*. Kincaid later married the editor's son, Allen Shawn, and they now have two children.

Kincaid has published four books: *At the Bottom of the River* (1992), a collection of short stories; *Annie John* (1989), a novel; *A Small Place* (1989), nonfiction; and *Lucy* (1991), a novel.

It was very difficult to set up an interview with Jamaica Kincaid. She was scheduled to speak at the Museum of Fine

Arts in Houston as part of a reading series, but weeks of effort trying to arrange the interview through her publisher had been to no avail. Finally, Fredrick Barthelme, the editor of *Mississippi Review*, said he could put in a good word for me to an editor at the *New Yorker*, and the day before Ms. Kincaid arrived her publicist said that she would indeed do the interview the day after her reading. We met February 13, 1991, in a large conference room off the main lobby of the very grand Wyndham Warwick Hotel. When Ms. Kincaid stepped off the elevator, I was struck by her appearance. A tall woman, she was dressed in what looked to be a Catholic schoolgirl's uniform: a plaid skirt, white blouse, white socks, and black shoes. Her hair was in pigtails, and she appeared to be a teenager even though she was over forty. I found her to be highly opinionated and steadfast in her beliefs, fiercely determined as to what she deemed morally correct and what she believed were social injustices. When the interview concluded, we went to eat Mexican food. She was very pleasant and interesting to talk with during our time together.

AV: Caribbean writer Derek Walcott, while writing about your work, stated that, "Genius has many surprises and one of them is geography." In what ways has geography both helped and hindered you as a writer?

JK: I can't say it has hindered me at all, and, if it has, I don't know of it. It seems to me that it has been more of a help since I can find nothing negative to say about the fact that I come from the place I'm from. I very much like coming from there. It would be false for me to take pride in it because it's an accident, really. It just seems to be sort of happenstance that I was born in this place and happenstance that I was born with black skin and all the other things I was born with. All that aside, the fact that I was born in this place, my geography has been, I think, a positive thing for me. I experience it as just fine. I am not particularly glad of it, as I say. The reality of my life is that I was born in this place. I find it only a help.

I can't say what it would have been like if I had been born a white Englishwoman. Actually, I think I *can* say. It seems as if it would have been quite wonderful because whenever I was growing up and looked at white English-women, they seemed to have a life denied me. This isn't to say if I had been born a white Englishwoman I would-n't have been perfectly miserable. They didn't seem per-fectly miserable; they seemed rather privileged and had all the things I couldn't have. I think I just made the best of what I had. What I had was my mother, my father, my mother's family, my father's family, all of that complica-tion, my history, which, as far as I know, began on boats. I'm part African, part Carib Indian, and part—which is a very small part by now—Scot. All of them came to Anti-gua by boats. This is how my history begins.

AV: The critic and black studies scholar Henry Louis "Skip" Gates, Jr., has stated about your work that "she never feels the necessity of claiming the existence of a black world or a female sensibility. She assumes them both. I think it's a distinct departure that she's making, and I think that more and more black American writers will assume their world the way that she does. So that we can get beyond the large theme of racism and get to the deeper themes of how black people love and cry and live and die. Which, after all, is what art is all about."

I agree with Gates' comment, but is this a conscious attempt by you not to overtly claim you are a black, female writer? Also, do you mind that you are still stereo-typed as a black, female, Caribbean writer?

JK: No, I thought what Skip said was very revealing for me because I did not know that I had been doing that. I come from a place where most of the people are black. Every important person in my life was a black person, or a person who was mostly black, or very deeply related to what we call a black person. So I just assume that is the norm and that it is the other people who would need describing. I assume most of the people who are important to me, and not last among them is my own self, are female. When I write about these people it would never occur to me to describe their race or their sex except as an aesthetic. I wouldn't say, "She has two eyes." I assume everyone has two eyes, and the only reason I would mention the eyes is if it were a superficial decision. It's not conscious at all that I leave out a people's race. Race is important, but the thing I know deeply is that when you say someone is white or black—in my case I never say anyone is black because I assume that to be the norm—because everybody has an idea of what that means. I never say people are white. I describe them. When you get to know people, you don't describe someone as "my wife that white woman." Or that man we just met [Kincaid is referring to a strange fellow who interrupted the taping of the interview for half an hour to pontificate his unusual views of the world], would you say, "He is a white man?" No, because what you would say is that he's a very intrusive person and that he was somewhat boorish, except we were sort of interested in his lunacy. So you look at him and immediately identify him as someone who is intrusive, and then from there you pick up on certain characteristics, but the least thing about him is that he's white.

To answer the second part of your question about being stereotyped, I think for the people who want to do it that it must be a very convenient way, but it really belittles the effort being made. When I sit at my typewriter I'm not a woman, I'm not from the Caribbean, I'm not black. I'm just this sort of unhappy person struggling to make something, struggling to be free. Yet the freedom isn't a political one or a public one: it's a personal one. It's a struggle I realize that will go on until the day that I die.

I'm living rather an ideal life. I think we all want to live a long life in which we attempt to be free. It's a paradox because the freedom only comes when you can no longer think, which is in death. You don't want to die, but you want to be free, and that's the outcome of the freedom. Perhaps I should say this is only a very personal view. In the meantime you struggle to make sense of the external from the things that have made you what you are and the things that you have been told are you: my history of colonialism, my history of slavery, and imagining if that hadn't happened what I would have been. Perhaps I would have been an unhappy woman in pre-European Africa. Who knows what I would have become? That's what I struggle to understand about myself.

It's not connected to the shell you see sitting at the typewriter. It's connected to the inner thing. Whatever I may say about being black, Caribbean, and female when I'm sitting down at the typewriter, I am not that. So I think it's sort of limited and stupid to call anyone by these names. The truth is, would we say John Keats is a white man who was a poet from nineteenth-century England? No, we just say he is John Keats. You think of these people in terms of their lives, and so that's what I'm saying. When you think of me, think of my life. My life is not a quota or an action to affirm an idea of equality. My life is my life. If it helps people to get to something I've written I'm glad, but, on the whole, I wish these terms would go away. Is my work any good? That is what I wish to know.

AV: Why was your childhood, which often serves as a basis for your stories, filled with sadness and anger when most readers would expect to find growing up on an island to be happy and carefree?

JK: I can say to most readers: try living on a Caribbean paradise and see if they find it happy and carefree. The thing I've learned is that all of life in every stage is hard to live. (How much more interesting it would have been for the world, not to mention less painful, if the Europeans in the fifteenth century had decided that the trouble with the part of the world they were in should be worked out within their borders.) Life is hard whether you live on a Caribbean island or somewhere else. No one living in these places you might think of as a paradise thinks it is paradise. They all want to leave. Even if someone could live the life of a tourist, no tourist goes to these places and wants to spend the rest of their life there. It was hard to grow up in a place like that, in particular because it doesn't have the comforts you think a place like that has. A person living in a place like that finds the sun hard to take. They find the nice days after awhile hard to take. After awhile it becomes a prison. Life is just extremely hard. I don't know of one person who lived in the West Indies as a child who thinks, "Oh, I always wish to remain a child in this wonderful atmosphere."

AV: In the magazine *W* you indicate that you dearly loved the St. John's library in Antigua, which closed in 1974 as a result of an earthquake: "Antigua used to be a place of standards. There was a sort of decency that it just doesn't have anymore," you said. "I think the tragedy of Antigua for me, when I began to see it again, was the loss of the library." You seem to see this event as being somehow symbolic of the state of your country. Does it apply to other countries as well?

JK: I hate to speak for other countries that have been and are in the situation Antigua is in, which is a former colony that is now independent. The sad fact is that they are all in the same boat. It's very hard to admit this, but they were all better off under colonial rule than they are now. This isn't to say that I want colonial rule back. I'm very glad to get rid of it. I'm only sad to observe that the main lesson we seem to have learned from colonial rule is all the corruption of it and none of the good things of it. We seem to have learned none of the good things about

Europe. I don't say "Western civilization" because I think this is a new term that implies white people and white superiorities. I now suspect when people refer to the greatness of Western civilization that they really mean the greatness of the white people of the world. So I'm not going to say that. What I'm going to say is that we learned none of the good things from Europeans—such as their love of education or their documenting the historical past, even if they lie about it, which they often do. Another great thing about the Europeans was their understanding of a community even if they violate it sometimes—no, they violated it all the time! They understood the idea of a community even as they limited it only to people who looked exactly like them. So that the French are excluded from the English idea of community and the Welsh are excluded and Scots are excluded and so on and so forth. Yet there are some great things Europeans had when they were among us, when they were ruling us, and one of them was education. The library in Antigua was a colonial institution and, had Antigua still been a colony when we had that earthquake, then the library would have been rebuilt and perhaps made better. So things like that are sad to admit, but we learned only the bad aspects. We have kept and refined all the bad aspects of the colonial power.

In Zimbabwe they have on their books laws that were put in place by the whites to oppress the blacks. The blacks, when they got power, kept those laws on the books and now use them against each other. In all of these places they practice oppressive political ideas. There is always a ruling power who behaves like the colonial power. They treat the citizens in the worst colonial way, but the only difference is that the countries are independent. We have no one to rebel against. There isn't any dividing line. It's like people in our own family doing these terrible things to you. They look like you. They're not white. They're not from far away. Yet they are behaving in the same way the colonial powers did.

So I come from one kind of corruption, the moral corruption of Europe, and now I find myself in a new kind of corruption. My background is that I am a product of corruption.

AV: There is a litany of items in "Girl" (from *At the Bottom of the River*) from a mother to her daughter about what to do and what *not* to do when it comes to being a nice young lady. Is this the way it was for you and other girls in Antigua?

JK: In a word, yes.

AV: Was that good or bad?

JK: I don't think it's the way I would tell my daughter, but as a mother I would tell her what I think would be best for her to be like. This mother in "Girl" was really just giving the girl an idea about the things she would need to be a self-possessed woman in the world.

AV: But you didn't take your mother's advice?

JK: No, because I had other ideas on how to be a self-possessed woman in the world. I didn't know that at the time. I only remember these things. What the mother in the story sees as aids to living in the world, the girl might see them as extraordinary oppression, which is one of the things I came to see.

AV: Almost like she's Mother England.

JK: I was just going to say that. I've come to see that I've worked through the relationship of the mother and the girl to a relationship between Europe and the place that I'm from, which is to say a relationship between the powerful and the powerless. The girl is powerless, and the mother is powerful. The mother shows her how to be in the world, but at the back of her mind, she thinks she never will get it. She's deeply skeptical that this child could ever grow up to be a self-possessed woman and, in the end, she reveals her skepticism; yet even within the skepticism are, of course, dismissal and scorn. So it's not unlike the relationship between the conquerer and the victim.

AV: What is the connection in the story "In The Night" between the jablesse and her night-soil father with the woman she wants to marry? Is the woman a jablesse?

JK: No. That story is really a portrait of night in Antigua. I don't remember it as being a story about a particular person. It's a portrait of a character within twenty-four hours.

AV: Why does the narrator skip from one sex to another in such stories as "In the Night" ("Now I am a girl, but one day I will marry a woman."), "At Last" ("Sometimes I appeared as a man."), and "Wingless" ("I myself have humped girls under my mother's house.")?

JK: In a way I can't answer that because I wouldn't want to explain it very much. I think when I was writing those stories I really wanted to disregard certain boundaries, certain conventions. These were stories written in my youth. (I think of the time before I had children as my youth.) These are stories in which I had endless amounts of time to consider all sorts of things and endless amounts of silence and space and distance. I could play with forms and identities and do things then that I can't do now because I don't have the time to plumb that kind of depth. They were attempts to discard conventions, my own conventions, and conventions that exist within writing. I still try to forget everything that I've read and just write. That was what that was about, and it really doesn't bear close interpretation from me. The reader would have to do that.

AV: You depict the most ordinary events. In the book *At the Bottom of the River*, are you trying to show that the most ordinary events can become extraordinary?

JK: Oh, yes! I think there is no such thing as an ordinary event. I believe everything is of the deepest significance. If you could isolate an event, it would lead to profound things. For example, if you would trace the ancestry of everybody who has crossed this room you wouldn't be able to do anything else.

AV: A number of your stories such as "What I Have Been Doing Lately," "Blackness," "My Mother," and *Annie John* (where the girl is sick and hallucinates over some pictures she is trying to clean) incorporate a type of magical realism. Are these phantasmagoric scenes derived from Latin American writers such as Borges or García Márquez, or even possibly Lewis Carroll?

JK: If it went back to anyone, it would be Lewis Carroll. Borges is the kind of writer when I read I'm just absolutely in heaven. I wouldn't say the same thing is true of García Márquez. I like reading him, but I don't feel it's the most wonderful thing like when I read Borges. The truth is, I come from a place that's very unreal. It's the reason for its political malaise, because it will not just look at the thing in front of it and act on it. The place I come from goes off into fantasy all the time so that every event is continually a spectacle and something you mull over, but not with any intention of changing it. It is just an entertainment. It's just some terrific thing you told yourself that happened today. I wouldn't say that I was influenced by these other writers you mentioned, because, for me, it's only an accident. It's really the place I grew up in. I'm not really a very imaginative writer, but the reality of my background is fantastic.

AV: You were born in 1949 as Elaine Potter Richardson, but in 1973 you adopted the pseudonym "Jamaica Kincaid." Was this name bestowed on you by George Trow of the *New Yorker*, and how was it chosen? You also stated that changing your name was a way of disguising yourself so you wouldn't have to be "the same person who had all these weights."

JK: No, by the time I met George Trow I had already changed my name. I wasn't that young. It's really more of the second question. I wanted to write. No one I knew had ever written. I thought serious writing was something people no longer did. By the time I discovered it was still being done, I didn't know how I could do it as the person who left home. I thought, and I think I would have been correct, I would have been judged pretentious. I would have been judged as someone stepping out of the things that had been established for me. I would have been laughed at. I didn't want anyone who knew me to know I was writing. I thought quite possibly my writing would be bad. The choosing of the name is something that is so private—because it also involves a lot of foolishness—that I can't even begin to tell you. It would involve remembering worlds of things that I remember quite well, but I'm no longer sure how to interpret what I was doing. I remember what I was doing, but I don't quite understand why I was doing it. So I'd rather not quite figure that out.

AV: If you don't want to answer the question directly, that's fine, but why "Jamaica" instead of "Antigua"?

JK: You see, you're trying to give it a logic that it did not have at the time. I was playing around with identities. When you're young you don't know how old you'll get to be and you feel every moment is *the* moment. In my case, there were many possibilities and that is the one I settled on. I had no idea anyone would one day be asking me how it all came to be or I would have made better sense of it at the time. I wanted to write, and I didn't know how. I thought if I changed my name and I wrote and it was very bad, then no one would know. I fully expected it to be bad, by the way, and to never be published, or heard from again. So I thought they'd never get to laugh at it because they wouldn't know it was me. So I changed my name. It was done one of those nights when you're sitting up late with friends who were trying out identities. If you saw photographs of me then, you would see how easy it was to do that. It was around this time I had started to write. When I started to get published no one ever called me Elaine. I'd always been unhappy with my name. You can almost say I became a writer just so I could change my name.

AV: Too English?

JK: No, the name Elaine always seemed stupid. (I hope there are not many Elaines out there.) At the time I changed it, I didn't know there were African names, although I don't think I could have done that because, by this time, I have as much connection to Africa as you do. The connection I have to Africa is the color of my skin, and that doesn't seem enough to have changed it to an African name. My new name unconsciously had the significance I wanted it to have since that is the area of the world I'm from. "Jamaica" is an English corruption of what Columbus called "Xaymaca." Kincaid just seemed to go together with Jamaica, but there were many combinations of names that could have been chosen one night when my friends and I were sitting around.

AV: You also stated that changing your name was a way of disguising yourself so that you wouldn't have to be "the same person who had all these weights."

JK: I could never lose the Elaine Potter Richardson identity, but I wanted to say things about the people in Antigua. I have met people, and they say I just can't talk about my family or friends in a bad way. This was a way to talk about things without people knowing it was me. I wanted to be able to be free of certain things. I wanted to speak truthfully about what I knew about myself without being myself. I suppose I had no idea it would have significance for anyone else.

AV: You left Antigua in 1966 when you were seventeen and moved to Westchester, New York. Why did you move, and was the decision yours alone?

JK: No. I left because of economic reasons. We thought I'd

be able to help my family by going away, to work and perhaps get an education. I come from a very poor family who worked very hard. At the time, my father was getting older and couldn't work as much as he used to. Actually, my education was cut short because I was supposed to go and help my family. I didn't go on to study at the university. I got to a certain level at school and was taken out so that I could come to America to work and help my family.

AV: So you didn't want to go to New York?

JK: No. I would have preferred to stay in school and gone on to university, but I was sent away. I was so depressed about what was happening to me. I wasn't going to be the person they thought I was going to be, which was one of these very uppity, ridiculous, university-educated women. Those type of women come back to Antigua and become school teachers, and they are very impressive, very important people in the community. I wasn't going to be like that. Instead, I was just going to be this supporter of my family and I was so miserable. Everyone said I was really very bright. So I didn't want to go, and I was very depressed, but it wasn't really my decision.

My decision would have been to be one of these very respected women who come back from the university and just sort of push everyone around. They are very well thought of. I wanted to be one of those. There is a certain kind of West Indian woman who's got great authority. All of them go to the University of the West Indies in Jamaica and become teachers or librarians. These are wonderful people who could run the world in a snap.

AV: It's lucky you didn't become a librarian, because you wouldn't have a job in Antigua.

JK: You're right—I wouldn't have a job. I probably would have gone to Canada. That's another thing that happens. All of these educated people in the West Indies can't find work there, so they go to Canada and the United States.

In Trinidad every Saturday there are people from American hospitals recruiting nurses. So Trinidad and places like that are robbed of their best nurses because the nurses get paid better here. In my case, I ended up going to Westchester because that was where I was going to be a nursemaid and go to school.

AV: *Annie John* appears to be an autobiographical novel. You have also stated (*New York Times Magazine*) that "lying is the beginning of fiction." Do you think fiction works best when reality is mixed with fiction?

JK: Well, I certainly can't make a fast rule about it and say that about everything. It seems to be that those things are true for me, so far, and I don't know what I'll do in the future. How I've written, so far, is to exploit my personal experiences. I have no idea of writing as an objective exercise. I only write about myself and about the people connected to me or the people I'm connected to.

I, for instance, could not write a marvelous novel as far as I know. I could not write even a very bad novel about someone living in Houston, Texas. I would not know how. I can only write about the things I know. I happen to be that sort of writer. The process of fiction, for me, is using reality and then reinventing reality, which is the most successful way to do what I do.

The part about "lying is the beginning of fiction" was true. I used to be accused when I was a little girl of having a strong imagination, and that was why I was a liar. I lied all the time. It was a way, I thought, of protecting my privacy. They tried to beat it out of me, sometimes literally, by giving me a spanking—no, a beating! (There is great cruelty to children in the West Indies.) I was always mistrusted. The only thing I was accused of was that I had a good memory. I never forgot anything that happened. I would hear people telling something that happened, and they would leave out, in my opinion, the crucial parts. Every part was crucial. If someone left something out, then I would tell what happened and they'd look at me in amazement. So my memory was considered an act of treachery, and I was asked not to have such a good memory. Essentially, I would be told that I should just forget certain things that happened. It was considered one of my greatest faults, but I'd remember everything and then I would invent things. For instance, if something happened, such as a little smoke coming out of a building and the fire truck came, then I would say, "Oh, it was the biggest fire you ever saw, and hundreds of fire trucks had to come." I was incapable of just describing something as it really happened. I would remember that it had happened, and I might exaggerate the details, but other people would forget it happened. So that is essentially what my fiction is. It really happened, but the details became exaggerated.

AV: Antigua appears to be paradise on the outside, but an evil lurks, embodied in the basket of green figs balanced on Annie's mother's head. The basket has a snake hidden within. Is this a biblical or a Conradian evil or something else altogether?

JK: It would be biblical, although these things are very unconscious, or subconscious. I did not know how much until very recently, when I began to just read my writing out loud and eventually just collected the images of my writing. I began to realize how my writing and my use of images are based on my own understanding of the world as good and evil as influenced by two books in the Bible, Genesis and Revelation. If that's all any writer has been influenced by, it would be enough. My understanding of the world is influenced very much by those two books, which were my favorite books to read from the Bible. I used to read the Bible as a child just for fun. I really loved reading it, especially Revelation, which I could not get enough of. I used to make myself afraid just by reading it. Do you know that part where it is the end of the world and they turn into rocks? I took it literally.

It became very real to me. So I'm very influenced by the

first book of the Old Testament and the last book of the New Testament. Everything in between is just sort of picturesque, but the beginning and end are the real thing. I did not know how much of an influence those biblical images had on my writing and understanding of the world until very recently.

It also turns out that there are recurring images of Lucifer, whom I apparently identify with, from *Paradise Lost*, which I did not know. I did not know how much I was rooting for the Devil.

AV: Would you also apply Lucifer's comment from *Paradise Lost*, "Better to reign in Hell, than serve in Heav'n," to Antigua's colonial situation?

JK: Yes. It is better to reign and to have self-possession in hell than to be a servant in heaven. You know how people would say, "Better red than dead"? I'm someone who would never say that. I always say, "It's better to be dead than to live like this. It's better to risk dying than to live as a slave." Always I say that.

AV: Is Annie John's love for Gwen supposed to be a substitution for her mother's lost love? Or are these lesbian tendencies?

JK: No, they weren't meant to be. I think I am always surprised that people interpret it so literally. The relationship between Gwen and Annie is really a practicing relationship. It's about how things work. It's like learning to walk. Always there is the sense that they would go on to lead heterosexual lives. Whatever happened between them, homosexuality would not be a serious thing because it is just practicing. The stories in *At The Bottom of the River* about the relationships between women are not meant, at least in my mind, to be homosexual. They were meant not to observe the convention of men and women, because I was trying to do away with certain conventions. I don't know if it comes up anyplace else, but Americans rather like to have things very much defined or to have things very much be what they say they are. The question of sexuality in these stories is not meant to be dwelt on because that is not the main thrust of them.

AV: There is a scene in *Annie John* where the narrator sees her reflection in a window yet doesn't recognize herself because she "had got so strange." Do you see yourself, both as a person and as a writer, still changing, or have the changes become less noticeable with age?

JK: By nature, I'm the sort of person who is never the same. Sometimes it's disturbing to me, because I find myself in a moment I like very much and wish I could stay that way, but I don't. I change very much. I'm still changing, but I don't always like it because it is not always convenient.

AV: Annie John's request to make a new trunk indicates she wants to start her own life, while the recovery from her illness as the long rain stops indicates she has moved from adolescence to womanhood. Is this correct?

JK: I think it is, but, again, at the time I was writing it, I wasn't conscious of these things as you point them out to me. If I were an objective reader, I'd be able to see it. I was writing these stories, and I was far less conscious of things than I am now. The sickness in the long rain actually happened when I was seven years old, with whooping cough, and I would get delirious. It's actually to that moment that I trace my fear of rodents. I was lying in my bed when I looked up and, around the edges of the ceiling that had this boarded mantel, I thought I saw hundreds of rats running around in a circle. I thought there were hundreds of them, but I think there was only one. I was powerless to do anything. I put that incident into the teenage life of the girl and made it a period of transition. I exaggerated the details.

AV: In *A Small Place*, you criticize tourists who go to Antigua to "escape the reality of their lives," which implies that tourists are an unthinking lot, and that tourists and their ancestors have profited from using Antigua. Isn't

this a generalization that is both unfair and discriminatory?

JK: Not at all. If you think it's unfair and discriminatory,
try it the other way around. Imagine that your existence
depended on people who are very different-looking than
you and whose differences seem to give them privileges
that you cannot even imagine. Just imagine the situation
in reverse. For example, in Vienna they depend mostly on
tourism. You and the Viennese look alike, so that aliena-
tion just isn't there, but even if you're a tourist among
people who look like you, they resent it. I can tell you
there are differences in going to Vienna and going to
Antigua. If you don't go to Vienna for fun, you can also
go to experience all of the cultural benefits and gain a
deeper understanding of the Western world. If you go to a
place like Antigua, it's to have a rubbish-like experience.
You want to forget who you are for the moment. You're
not interested in these people. You're not interested in
their culture, except in some sort of anthropological way
that offers you psychic relief. They have nothing of value
you want to bring home. It's an escape, a moment to
forget who you really are. If you think there isn't anything wrong with it, then try living it and you'll see how
quickly you want to shoot every tourist you ever meet.
It's deeply wrong.

AV: The Antigua you grew up in no longer exists, but it is
the one you love. Still, you wrote a scathing diatribe
against the English for trying to make Antigua English.
Yet now the English are gone and you hate Antigua even
more. Why?

JK: The question isn't whether the current system doesn't
work, so let's bring the old system back. The English
were wrong when they were there, and it is wrong today.
I think, dare I pat myself on the back, that it's very good
that I'm able to admit that we've made a mess of things. I
don't wish the British to come back. I wish the British to

stay in Britain. I wish everyone would stay where they came from because when we go to other places—no matter if we say you go to extend your influence—you eventually exploit. Antigua is in terrible shape, and it should be changed into something better. It's not a question of degrees of morality, but simply just morality. Just because Antiguans behave like fools doesn't mean that we should have other people who are also fools.

AV: You say that Antiguans who graduate from the Hotel Training School are nothing better than contemporary slaves who wait on tourists. Isn't this extending the metaphor a bit far? After all, aren't they free to choose to work for a hotel and to have the right to earn income?

JK: Antigua used to have a teacher's training college of which we were all proud, but it seems it was a peculiar choice to change a teacher's college to a school for graduating hotel employees. First of all, have you ever heard of anything more ridiculous? I don't believe Italians or French go to training school to be waiters, or even if there is such a thing as a training school because it's something anyone can do. If you have to go to a training school, then there must be something desperately wrong. We're not talking about a scientist or a brain surgeon. We are talking about putting a pineapple on a table. If you need to go to school to learn how to do this, then what are we really talking about?

I can't see there is a sense of freedom because that seems to be the wrong word. It implies you are free to be a hotel waiter or to starve. I know how to set a table. I did that in Brownie meetings. These are things everyone knows how to do. If you don't know how to bend and kiss behinds, do you mean you are going to school for that?

I don't mean to take lightly the institution of slavery, but it seems to me the mentality of these small islands is very much related to slavery. These island rulers are

pretentious since they pretend their little islands are nations. Back home they talk about the nation of Antigua,
but it's only a stupid little island. If they'd only do something ordinary and logical such as educating their citizens
that would be fine, but you don't want them to pretend
and be something they are not. The fact is, they don't
even do the things that a small village in the U.S. would
try to do.

AV: You live in America, you are married to an American,
and you are published by an American publisher; yet you
continue to use English spellings (e.g., "colour" instead
of the Americanized "color"). Why?

JK: I've lived in America longer than I've lived in Antigua. I
lived in Antigua sixteen years, and I'm now forty-two.
From the time I was seventeen to now, it has been twenty-
five years I've lived in America. When I talk about going
home, my husband says, "What home are you talking
about?" I think of Antigua as my home. I'm not an
American citizen. I haven't become an American because
I don't think America needs another writer. Antigua
needs a writer more than it needs an American citizen. I
have no intention of becoming an American citizen. My
children are American and they can say the Pledge of
Allegiance just like my husband can, but they don't have
to say it because they're Americans. No American has to
say it.

AV: What has been Antigua's response to your book *A
Small Place*? I can't imagine the government looks upon
you favorably.

JK: I think about that all the time. I imagine that I'd be shot.
I haven't been back since the book was published. I
wanted to go this year, but I didn't want to be separated
from my children. I booked a flight the day the war in
Iraq started; yet I didn't know how it would turn out, and
I decided not to go. Now I don't have the time. God
knows if they would shoot me, but it's a criminal place. I

wouldn't be surprised if they had henchmen who would do it, because politics in the West Indies is very tribal. People take their colors very seriously. They divide themselves into people who wear red and who wear blue.

My mother is a blue. I'm nothing. When I was growing up, we were reds. Then my mother joined the party that broke away, and they are blue. She takes it so seriously. For example, I bought her a red T-shirt and she said, "No, I could never wear that." Even though she was visiting me in the United States, she brought her loyalties with her. This makes you think there isn't any hope for people in Antigua who think like this.

AV: The character Lucy appears to be similar to Annie John, except she is a few years older. Did you consider keeping the name "Annie John" for this character?

JK: I don't consider it a continuation because I would never write like that. It's a continuation only in the sense that it's about my life and it's the same life I'm writing about, but they weren't meant to be the same person at all. In any case, a key to Lucy is the name Lucifer and so she couldn't be called Annie at all. It's a very shallow— though understandable—connection to make, because the reader isn't me and in my mind, observing what I'm doing. I'm not interested in making the thing whole. I'm interested in parts of things. When Annie left her mother, that was it. We're not going to hear from Annie again. We're not going to hear from Lucy again. You might very well hear about a woman's life in the metropolitan area of the world, whether it's London, New York, Toronto, or wherever.

You might very well hear about how this life turned out, but to say it's a continuation of Lucy would be a mistake. Very, very crucial to understanding Lucy is her name. I think most people in America have such a different background than I do that people in America, especially in universities, are so obsessed with race that they miss the crucial things about Lucy. The great influences on that young woman's life are Genesis and Revelation and, strangely enough, *Jane Eyre*. I think all sorts of things escape American readers.

I suppose my writing is as mysterious to an American reader as someone like Zora Neal Hurston is to me. She's a woman who wrote in the twenties, part of the Harlem Renaissance, who had a very brilliant career and then died a maid in poverty. It's one of those stories which either you think is an American story or you think it is a racial story, but those are things that to really understand what I'm trying to do you'd have to know. Lucy is a very moralistic person, and she's very judgmental, because her view of the world is very much shaped by a nineteenth-century view.

AV: The scene in which Lucy tells her dream to Lewis and Mariah is uncomfortable because the couple looks at the dream from a Freudian and sexual viewpoint, whereas Lucy interprets it as meaning she has accepted them into her life. Did you have something like this happen to you in real life?

JK: Well, that I will not say. The scene really explains itself, because the people had become real to her. If you show up in someone's dream, it means they are finally real to you. It's a cultural gap. I tried to show that Lucy did not understand it; she only reports what happened in her dream. Of course, I understand it, but Lucy doesn't and isn't quite clear about it. Lucy doesn't know who Dr. Freud is, and it's said with a certain simplicity. I think it's the sort of thing I wouldn't have been able to write five years ago. I wouldn't have been able to separate the knowledge I have of Freud from the knowledge I did not have.

AV: There is the contrast between the island girl, Sylvie, who has the teethbite mark on her cheek, and Mariah, who "looked blessed, no blemish or mark of any kind on her cheek or anywhere else." Lucy does not identify with pleasant-smelling Mariah; she prefers to have a powerful odor. Why is Lucy, as well as Annie John, so iconoclastic? She seems to rebel against most things that are good, yet she has no reason to act this way.

JK: I think it's that "reign in hell, serve in heaven" problem again. A person like Sylvie seems more self-possessed to her. Even in her embryonic consciousness-raising, she knows that it's better from a feeling of self-possession to be Sylvie rather than Mariah, spiritually speaking. There's something sad about Mariah and, ultimately, defeated. She's the victim among the conquerors, whereas Sylvie is the victor among the defeated.

Later on, Lucy develops sympathy and grows to love Mariah. Lucy is the sort of person who, no matter what happens to her, would never identify with the victors. Lucy is naive, but she is not stupid.

Mariah is a lovely person. She didn't think the world would turn on her. What undoes Mariah is trusting in human nature, but this is not possible for Lucy, who trusts and mistrusts at once. It's not the sort of thing Mariah would understand, because she thinks love is all. Lucy thinks love is fine, but she doesn't look upon love as an absolute reality.

AV: Mariah shows Lucy the daffodils in the garden, but Lucy wants to kill the flowers. Why do so many of your characters have such negative, conflicting feelings?

JK: Let me answer that in a roundabout sort of way. My husband and I went to Paris last September on a boat. We sailed on the *QEII*, and after we arrived at Southampton we spent a couple of days in London. Every time I go to England I almost have a nervous breakdown. I have such conflicting feelings of England. I love it, and I hate it. It's not possible for me to be a tourist. I realize I'm a visitor, but when I go to England, what happens is that I also confront my past.

AV: It's ironic the English were waiting on you.

JK: Yes, that's true, although there weren't many English waiting on me. They were Pakistani, Irish, and Africans, but not many English were waiting on me. So we stayed in London and took a train to Dover where we were going to catch a ferry. We were getting to Dover, and I couldn't believe what my eyes were seeing: the White Cliffs of Dover! I had yet another nervous breakdown that was quite like Lucy and those daffodils. I had heard so much about those white cliffs. I used to sing a hymn in church that was about longing to see the White Cliffs of Dover over and over again. Things like that permeate my memory, but these things have absolutely no value to me. I hardly know the names of any flowers growing in the West Indies, except the hibiscus, but I know the names of just about all the flowers in England and I also can identify them. There is something very wrong here when I know the name of each flowering bush growing in England, but not in Antigua. I know the White Cliffs of Dover, and I've yearned for them. I could have lived a millennium without ever seeing them. So there is something wrong there, just as it would have been false for a person like Lucy to love those daffodils. Daffodils do not grow in tropical climates. I know a poem about daffodils, but I did not know a poem about hibiscus.

AV: Was there resentment after seeing the White Cliffs of Dover?

JK: Yes, of course there is resentment.

AV: But aren't the White Cliffs really amazing?

JK: They *are* amazing. They really are amazing.

AV: Lucy identifies with the French painter Gauguin, who found his homeland to be a prison and wanted something different. The two are much alike, even though Gauguin escaped to the islands while Lucy left the islands. Do you feel much in common with Gauguin, whose painting *Poèmes Barbares* is the cover picture for *Lucy*?

JK: I hesitate to say I identify with this man. I must say, as I was writing parts of *Lucy*, I was reading one of his journals called *The Intimate Journals of Paul Gauguin*. I found it a great comfort because he was so unrelenting of himself. He was very selfish and very determined; yet there are two things that struck me in that book. The first thing that struck me is his account of his friendship with van Gogh, which is the most hilarious yet cruel thing I've ever read. I never have laughed so much in jest. He describes van Gogh cutting off his ear, and you are just aghast because it's all very astonishing. The second thing was when he asked Strindberg to write an introduction to one of his shows. Strindberg wrote back a very long letter saying why he could not do it because he disliked Gauguin's work. So Gauguin used the letter as the introduction even though the letter stated what was bad about his paintings. Gauguin wasn't afraid to use someone's negative view of his work. He wore it as a badge. I rather admire that.

So I think the criticism I most value comes from people who do not like my writing. There's almost nothing that makes you feel more superior than the people who don't like you.

AV: The narrators or main characters of your fiction seem to have a cursory or dispassionate regard for sex (such as in the chapter titled "The Tongue" in *Lucy*). What was your viewpoint of sex as a young woman, and how has it changed as you've grown older?

JK: Good heavens, I don't think I could answer the first part of the question, although I must say Lucy rather enjoys it. What Lucy doesn't want is to be possessed again. She has just escaped a certain possession from her mother, and she doesn't want to be possessed again. I think at the end of the book she wishes she could be possessed and loved, but she can't at this point in her life. I suppose what she is saying is that she wishes time would pass quickly to allow herself to be consumed.

AV: Your writing style in *Lucy* is somewhat unusual in that you often start a passage, but before it is fully developed, you digress to a previous experience. For example, there is the party at Paul's where Peggy disapproves of Paul, but then you digress to the story of Myrna and Mr. Thomas on the island.

JK: It's not anything deliberate, but last night after my reading someone said they really admired the way I had done that scene. It sort of leads you to explain how something was written, but I've come to understand there is no such thing in writing as a technique. Quite often you invent what you're doing while you're doing it, and it would be quite wrong to apply that style to all my writing. I was not aware of any special thing when I did that. I did that in *Lucy,* and that was it, but I have no intention of using it again. If it were to turn up again, it would be because I felt that was what was needed.

AV: With each book, your characters gain both insight and maturity with age, culminating with the ability to possibly love. Will your next book develop along these same lines, or do you plan to take off in a different direction?

JK: I really cannot say. For me, writing is a revelation. If I knew what it would be, then it would be of no interest for me to do it. When I sit down to write, I will reveal to myself what I already know. I already know all of this. I know how it works, but I haven't quite said it yet. The minute that I'm conscious of it, then it's of no interest. When I sit down to write it, it will become conscious to me. I will know it, and then I will move on. So I don't know what will happen. I don't know how it will work.

AV: What are your thoughts about interviews? In what ways are they good or bad? Do interviews help you understand yourself and your writing by openly discussing your work?

JK: I forget interviews once they are done. The two or three times I've been interviewed, I have read what I've said when I edit it, but I'm shocked that I've said these things.

I find that some of my responses sound very intelligent, or they may sound very stupid. I can't believe it's me. So I just simply forget it. I never listen to myself on the radio. I've been on television once, but I would never watch myself! Doing this interview is like having a conversation, but later I will just forget it. It's of no help, and it's of no hindrance.

AV: In the past twenty years, your life has changed dramatically. Do you have a different perspective of the world now than you had back when you were an *au pair*?

JK: Yes, and it's not good. No, it's worse than I thought. The world is not a better place than when I was a servant. It's true if I'd gone to England I would have remained a servant, and it was only by sheer chance that I came to America. I'm really glad I did come to America, which is a place that has allowed me to denounce it. I think it's to America's credit that it can spawn someone like me. I like living in America because it gives me the language and the idea to rearrange the world in what I'd think would be a just equation. I can't say that my perspective has changed. I think, by now, I'm supposed to be a Republican. I'm supposed to be someone who says, "Yes, the system works." But actually I'm someone who says, "I'm not sure that it works." I suppose if my perspective has changed it would be that I'm now a politically conscious person. To America's credit, I've become—at least verbally—a politically conscious person. I suspect that if I wasn't writing, being the person I am who has become politically conscious, then I would be throwing bombs. If I didn't have the pen, I would certainly be someone who would take up the sword.

A Hard Kind of Play

AN INTERVIEW WITH

Ron Hansen

R$_{ON}$ H$_{ANSEN}$ was born in Omaha, Nebraska, and received a B.A. in English literature from Creighton University in 1970. Later, at the Iowa Writers' Workshop, he studied with John Irving, and then received the Wallace Stegner Creative Writing Fellowship at Stanford, where he studied with John L'Heureux and completed *Desperadoes*. *Desperadoes*, a historical novel about the Dalton gang, received great critical acclaim; *The New York Times Book Review* went so far as to list Hansen as one of the five best new writers in 1979.

He went on to write *The Assassination of Jesse James by the Coward Robert Ford*, which was published in 1983 and finished as runner-up for the William Faulkner Award.

In 1987 Hansen published two books: *The Shadow-maker*, a highly praised children's book, and *You Don't Know What Love Is*, an anthology of contemporary American fiction. His own short stories were collected and published in a volume titled *Nebraska* in 1989, the same year that the American Academy and Institute of Arts and Letters presented him with an award in literature. His most recent novel, *Mariette in Ecstasy*, was chosen by the *Nation* as one of the best books in 1992. Hansen chairs the creative writing program at the University of California, Santa Cruz. He has written screenplays for all three of his novels, and all three are slated to be made into major motion pictures within the next year or two.

The interview was conducted in the summer of 1984, just before he returned to the Iowa Writers' Workshop as a visiting professor. I sent him a letter containing twenty questions while he was living in San Francisco. Within a week, I received, to my amazement, his responses to all my questions. Aside from the interview, Ron and I had only sporadic contact until we finally met at our twenty-fifth high school reunion in Omaha in 1991. I later had the privilege to review *Mariette in Ecstasy* for the *Bloomsbury Review*, whereupon he amended our interview with an update about his latest novel.

AV: I recall that you were listed in 1979 by the *New York Times Book Review* as one of the five best new writers of the year when *Desperadoes* was published. Yet the road to critical success had its bumps. Can you trace your educational background as well as some of the jobs you had before the publication of *Desperadoes*?

RH: I've been tinkering with fiction ever since grade school, so I feel I've had a long apprenticeship in the writer's craft even though I'm just getting used to my thirties. My high school years at Creighton Preparatory School were those of many an Omaha boy, as were my years at Creighton University, except that I edited and contributed to the literary magazine and was the newspaper's political cartoonist. I sought escape from the Great Plains by accepting a commission as a second lieutenant in the army. I thought I could write about the Vietnam conflict as Crane, Hemingway, and Mailer had written about other wars—the notion seemed neither callow nor preposterous then—but instead I served two years in southern Arizona, where I was the senior officer in the casualty branch. I notified next-of-kin about their missing or dead in Asia, I escorted returning corpses to funeral homes, I oversaw burials, and in order to remove myself from that saddening work, I wrote short stories in my room—one was a prize winner in the Armed Forces Short Story Writing Contest—or I took flying lessons, played tennis, read deeply in American history.

It was the stories that sent me to the Iowa Writers' Workshop where I studied under John Irving and, for one semester, John Cheever. I earned a fellowship and a teaching assistantship in literature and completed a master of fine arts thesis entitled "No Cares Have I To Grieve Me," a fictional memoir that was so apparently influenced by Frank Conroy's masterpiece *Stop-Time* and so unprotected in its revelations that I have since locked the book away until the time comes when I can read it without pain.

Following graduation in 1974, I attended the Cummington Community of the Arts on a summer scholarship, and thereafter worked at a number of jobs, among them housepainter, leasing agent, jack-of-all-trades, while toiling at night and on weekends at fiction. I sold stories to *The Little Magazine, Carolina Quarterly,* and *The Iowa Review*—none of the stories much like the one that preceded it—but my real concentration was a novel about my army service, a novel called *The Escort.* It was not an entertainment. It was as serious and surly as any book ever submitted, and I recalled it from the marketplace when I saw each editor's rejection contained a synonym for "grim."

I got a job selling college textbooks in Illinois, Indiana, and St. Louis, and in the late afternoons I would return to my motel room and scratch away at a novel that was not about me or even about the puzzling twentieth century, but about an outlaw gang in 1890s Oklahoma. I wrote as always in pencil and in a large black book of blank pages, carrying it with me like letters from home. And I can still recall writing *Desperadoes* with all the zest of a man who feels good fortune is just around the corner. And I reached that corner in April 1977: I sold another story to *The Iowa*

Review, I learned I was a winner in the *Penthouse Magazine* New Writers Short Story Contest, and I was given a Wallace Stegner Creative Writing Fellowship at Stanford University. I moved to California and wrote a story about a salesman that the *Atlantic Monthly* published, and I revised my novel about the Dalton brothers with the canny advice of John L'Heureux, director of the creative writing program at Stanford. I sent *Desperadoes* to Robert Gottlieb at Alfred A. Knopf, who read it over the weekend and bought it on Monday. And it was a nice coincidence that on that same night I was hired to teach basic and advanced fiction writing at Stanford as a Jones lecturer. And it has been writing or teaching that has occupied my time ever since.

AV: Most contemporary writers choose to experiment with their particular narrative style in a contemporary setting, yet you decided upon historical fiction for your first two novels.

RH: Many contemporary writers use contemporary settings because they want to explain their own lives or speak about what is important to them, a subject or problem that usually came up just recently. I'm really too private for that sort of exploration—I suppose the closest I'll ever get to my own life is my master's thesis at Iowa, a series of linked stories about a character who was very much like myself. Even there, however, the relationship between "Jack Baker" and myself is many degrees away from the parallel. Historical fiction gave me the opportunity to say all I knew about the West and about philosophical questions I thought were important, and it kept me away from a contemporary world that I find comparatively boring. And I liked the idea of using a popular genre, such as the Western or the historical novel, as a way of expanding the appeal of my work to people who wouldn't normally pick it up.

AV: In *Desperadoes*, Emmett Dalton's elderly reminiscence

of the Dalton gang reminded me of the structure of Thomas Berger's *Little Big Man*, a recollection by Jack Crabb. Did Berger's book influence you?

RH: Yep. I came across *Little Big Man* in a paperback edition in 1970, and it was love at first sight, a superb book, and though I purposely didn't reread it prior to writing *Desperadoes,* Thomas Berger's great novel was very much on my mind during the composition.

AV: Throughout *Desperadoes* and *The Assassination of Jesse James by the Coward Robert Ford* the reader cannot help but notice the language, which is historically accurate, and your choice of words, which is remarkably descriptive. For example, on the first page of *Jesse James* you write, "a rope swing looped down from a dying elm tree and the ground below it was scuffed soft as flour." To what do you attribute your writing style?

RH: You develop a writing style—at least when you're young—by imitating the styles of those published writers you most appreciate. I began with the greatest affinity for the work of John Updike and have learned from writers as unalike as Ernest Hemingway and Elizabeth Bishop, as E.L. Doctorow and Norman Mailer, as William H. Gass and Thomas McGuane. I was a painter as a boy, and I liken my style to a painterly one, with emphasis on color, comparison, and metaphor. I'm uncomfortable with abstractions and generalities and vagueness, and what I'm conscious of, as I'm writing, is of putting words down that will somehow convince me of the reality of the scene I'm trying to render. William Gass once said he couldn't read contemporary poetry because the words slide right off the page—a comment I interpret to mean too little attention is paid to imagery and heightened language, and the plainness of much of contemporary writing in America threatens to make our literature imprecise, inarticulate, and as easy to forget as yesterday's noodle soup. Historical accuracy is important to me because I want my characters to be at ease inside my paragraphs, but descriptive writing is important to me because it pleases me to reread it.

AV: Although your first two novels share a common theme of Old West outlaws who meet a tragic fate, there is a distinct difference between the lighter side of *Desperadoes* and the darker side of *Jesse James*. Why?

RH: I would have been repeating myself if I told the James gang story as I did the Dalton gang, and I wanted to correct the impression that approved of the empty-headed notion that these criminals were expressing something important about America. *Desperadoes* was a joy to write, *Jesse James* was a job. But I didn't want to produce a popular entertainment, but the deepest book I had in me at the time. There are sentences, and even pages, in *Jesse James* that I'm very proud of, but it's a hard book even for me to love; the penance is there in every word.

AV: Bob Ford and Jesse James seem to evoke the Doppelganger motif as Nabokov used it in his novels *Lolita*, *Pale Fire*, and *Despair*. Is this a fair assessment?

RH: I agree that the Doppelganger principle is at work in the novel, but Nabokov is simply too foreign for me to think of in the context of Jesse James. Joseph Conrad, perhaps. There's a great deal of *The Secret Sharer* in the relationship between Jesse and Bob. I was blithely writing one scene in which Jesse and Bob were at a dining room table and, for some reason having to do with this idea of the Doppelganger, one of my characters urged Bob to list all of the things that he and Jesse had in common. Bob and I started listing those things together, and I was frankly surprised by how long the paragraph was getting. From this I got a new appreciation of why Jesse James—who was otherwise so protective—would allow this disciple into his home. He says to Bob at one point, "I figure if I can get you right I'll be just that much closer to me." My best explanation for Jesse permitting Bob Ford to come to St. Joseph, and for Bob Ford's courting of Jesse James, is that they both saw in each other a counterpart, a spirit in harmony with his own.

AV: Of course, such a realization reflects the process of character invention, which raises the issue of how to reconcile the historical aspects of the work with the fictive aspects. When you research a historical novel what are your basic sources and what steps do you take? Any interesting stories you could share about visiting these small midwestern towns where the Dalton and James gangs rode nearly a hundred years ago?

RH: The steps I take for writing historical fiction are pretty much the steps I take for writing contemporary fiction. I read virtually everything that has any relationship to the subject at hand, read more deeply as the writing progresses, go to movies that handle the same themes, and compare my work with other novels of the period. Interviews with relatives are usually disappointing—for example, how much do you really know about your grandmother? And visits to Coffeyville, Kansas, and St. Joseph, Missouri, were helpful only inasmuch as they gave me a chance to see a good many photographs of the Daltons and the Jameses. I use photographs, to a great extent, and also maps, dictionaries of idiom and American slang, and graphs that remind me of birthdates, eye color, handicaps, and characteristic phrases. Somewhere between all this factual and semi-factual information—and my imagination of the way these people were based on the knowledge I have of them—the story emerges as a kind of balance between my individual assessment of the characters and their actions as recorded by those alive at the time.

AV: Historical fiction seems to take advantage of the old adage "truth is stranger than fiction." Perhaps we sometimes find historical fiction more engrossing than so-called "pure" fiction because we know the events depicted have in some sense happened. In that regard, it's ironic that the Daltons were once lawmen and that, with the exception of Grat, the Dalton brothers did not seem evil. Rather, they were simply poor, lazy cowboys who preferred theft to ranchwork. They became prisoners of the events that happened to them. Is this the way it really was?

RH: A good many apologists for Old West outlaws try to extenuate crimes with claims of poverty, but, of course, many people were poor back then but only a few became thieves. I composed *Desperadoes* and *The Assassination of Jesse James by the Coward Robert Ford* with the benefit of some fine scholarship on crime that has been published lately, and I used some conclusions about contemporary outlawry in writing about the past. In the same way that rapists are not really after sexual gratification but use rape as an expression of power, many thieves do not really need the money, many killers feel no hate for their particular victims, and many people who are in jail deny they've done anything wrong. Emmett Dalton certainly did, and it's because Emmett narrates *Desperadoes* that it works as an entertainment. You like the gang more than you ought to. When I decided to do a companion book about Jesse James and Robert Ford, I decided to write it in an omniscient voice so readers could see the criminals as history does. I adopted a documentary style and the unsurprised-by-anything tone of a nineteenth-century god in order to convince my readers that this was exactly what was going on back then, and not the gentlemanly things they'd imagined from movies.

AV: Speaking of movies, I understand that work is under way on screenplays for both *Desperadoes* and *Jesse James*. Aren't you concerned that the printed word will lose that built-in tension and effectiveness, that implicit reality, when transcribed to celluloid?

RH: You can't be certain about a film's effectiveness in the way you can be certain about a book's, mostly because so many people have a hand in the final product. As for what happens to a book once it's made into a film, I like James M. Cain's reply. A reporter once asked Cain if Cain approved of what Hollywood had done to *The Postman Always Rings Twice* and *Double Indemnity* and *Mildred Pierce*. Cain pointed a finger toward his bookshelves and said, "Hollywood hasn't done anything to them; they're all sitting right there." You can't expect a movie to repeat every aspect of a book; you can only hope that the movie suggests some of the overriding ideas and that people are moved enough to go back to the prose.

AV: To return to the development of your prose, in the dedication to *Jesse James* you list three people named John: Irving, L'Heureux, and Gardner. What influence have these three writers had on you?

RH: I give a lot of thought to dedications—I guess most writers do—and sentimentality is my last consideration. I look for some connection with the novel's material, with what I was trying to get across. My father died during the writing of *Jesse James*, and for some time the book was dedicated to him, but I couldn't remember him ever mentioning the James boys, and I hope someday to get a project that will tell the story of my mother's and father's relationship, so that dedication for him is still forthcoming.

John Gardner worked with the *James* manuscript over three Bread Loaf Writers' conferences, giving the book a great amount of attention, giving me great advice. I'd made preparations to go to his wedding to Susan Thornton when he had his motorcycle accident. I planned to dedicate the book to his memory in appreciation for his help, and then I considered the subject matter of the novel and what was, in Jesse James and Bob Ford, a perverse master-and-pupil relationship. My own experiences with writing teachers were exceptionally positive, and if John Gardner expressed all that was good in a teaching relationship, so did John Irving, with whom I studied at Iowa, and John L'Heureux, with whom I studied and worked at Stanford. I thought of that dedication as a way of thanking three good men for their help and support, and also as a way of honoring the teaching profession.

AV: Since you have taught and are teaching creative writing on the university level, perhaps you could discuss some of the advantages and disadvantages of being a teacher/writer—or is it a writer/teacher?

RH: I miss teaching when I'm away from it, and when I'm at it I find I'm always looking for ways to get away from it again. I find it appealing, compelling, frequently overwhelming, inspiring, disappointing, depressing, and generally invigorating. The problem is that a good writing teacher is doing pretty much what a good writer does, but he's doing it for other people who may or may not accept his ideas. You're called upon to rewrite sentences, reimagine scenes, suggest other plot developments, pinpoint weaknesses, punch up dialogue, and much of the time while you're doing that you've got a manuscript of your own that needs to have its sentences rewritten, its scenes reimagined, its dialogue punched up. I once taught a course at Michigan that met only once a week, on a Wednesday night, so that I could spend the other six and a half days per week on my own work. And yet, on Wednesday, at two or three in the afternoon when I really had to begin preparing for class, I'd be filled with anger over giving up those hours when I could be going ahead with my novel. On the other hand, there was a period when my novel was as plain and simple as cheese and nothing I did made it jump, and I was called up and offered a course that I loved every minute of. My students were princes and princesses. Their stories would have made Chekhov weep, golden sunlight filled the room, and if I went to my manuscript and it simply stayed in its place like old pudding, well, I was teaching now and could put the writing off. And, in fact, I went back to the novel with fresh insights about what was right with it and what was wrong. The teaching of writing forces you to say things about grammar, style, characterization, and design that you may forget as you're pushing words around. Going back to a novel after a class often has the effect, for me, of giving instructions to myself, of rehearing what I said to some poor soul yesterday and realizing that it was my subconscious speaking and that the words were meant only for me. I'm making myself sound like a slipshod teacher, but I think I'm a pretty good one if only because I'm as deeply involved in the subject at hand as my students are. Our energies generate us, and we go out of the classroom with a feeling of excitement about what we're going to say next. When I'm in my house and the page won't get better, the only thing I can do is keep at it. I sometimes wind up looking at the phone and hoping it will ring—anything that will pull me away from my own misbegotten prose. Right now I can't imagine not teaching; it's good for my writing, my peace of mind, and I hope it's helpful for my students.

AV: In this regard, most of your students start out writing and submitting short stories, as did you. You recently had a short story published in *Esquire* titled "True Romance." How did this story evolve, and have you published any other short pieces?

RH: I've been writing short stories for a long time but only get to publishing one out of every four or five that I complete. I write some very quickly and in a spirit of whimsy. Good judgment prevents me from mailing them out. Others have been published over such a space of time, and in such little-read publications that very few people, perhaps only myself, could have seen all of them—ten, at present. The stories have been collected together and will be published under the title *Nebraska*.

"True Romance," the short story, had its origins in

1975 when I was living on a lake that was close to
Columbus, Nebraska. A stockyard and auction barn
were close by, and I'd see young farmers who didn't fit at
all the world's image of good men of the soil. I thought at
times about writing an article about them, but journalism is something I can easily pass up. About this time
there were some cattle mutilations and a good number of
theories explaining them, including devil worshippers
and close encounters of the second kind. And there was a
week in my life when I was at a fishing resort and it was
raining perpetually. I kept to myself on a screened porch
of the main lodge and read anything I picked up. As it
happened, all I picked up were confessions magazines. I
kept waiting for their article's narrators to break up into
laughter but they remained fascinatingly sober about
their petty and crazily complicated lives. So, in desperation, one rainy day in a fishing lodge in 1975, I began a
short story about young farmers whose cattle are being
mutilated and they don't know why or by whom. And
there I stopped. I didn't know what would happen next,
but there was a paragraph or two that I liked, so I kept
the pages. About once a year I'd go back to that story,
and, eventually, I came up with a long, very zany piece
about a monster who spoke in gobbledygook. I rewrote
that story completely, making it a simple horror story
that could have been a teleplay for "The Twilight Zone."
I went back to my original conception and made the style
closer to that of poker-faced comedy, working in more
about soap operas, confessions magazines, all those distancing mechanisms that keep people from seeing the
real horror in their lives. And I came up with a peculiar
story called "True Romance" that I really don't expect
people to understand completely since I'm a little up in
the air about it myself.

My methods are pretty much the same for every story—
it's always happenstance, putting together, delaying, re-

writing, putting away, picking it up again until the story is nearly presentable and I can slap a postage stamp on it.

AV: Could you elaborate further on your writing habits or disciplines?

RH: I get up at six-thirty or seven, read the morning newspaper with a pot of coffee, read or reread some poetry, and by eight-thirty usually get around to opening up my blank book and picking up my pencil. I don't know why I have to trick myself in this way, because usually, once I get the pencil in my hand, the words start spilling out and my main job is to cross out one or give some thought to another or to check the dictionary to see if this word's proper meaning is the one I want. Often I'm looking for both practical sense and euphony, and there are some quirks I have that hamper my writing process—my own kind of discipline—but I won't go into them for fear of appearing crazy. I may quit at noon for lunch and come back for another two hours in the afternoon, or I may go on until four o'clock and then run in a nearby park. I'm surprised, when I count up the hours, that I have so few pages at the end of the day.

AV: But the number of pages is only one by-product of your method; meaningful prose seems to take on a higher order of importance because you work slowly. Since you were a student and clearly an admirer of John Gardner, do you agree with his contention that fiction should have a moral point of view?

RH: *On Moral Fiction* has engendered a good many arguments, particularly because of the arrogance of a chapter in which Gardner points out those writers of whom he approves and those he does not. You'd have to know John Gardner to know that he was playing the rogue in parts of that book, that there was an impishness, a wink of the eye, in many of his most upsetting statements. He was a man who, in the most good-hearted way, would call a person stupid, an idea goofy, and, in class, get away with it because his caring and sympathy were always so apparent. In print, his words seemed vituperative and preachy, and for that reason the book was probably a mistake.

I buy the premise of it, however. And that premise appears to me to be that all great fiction is moral; that is, all great fiction pretends that human beings have the will power to do good or evil, that ideas have consequences, and that existence matters. I've read some people's complaints that Gardner's thesis would pitch out as junk most of Shakespeare's plays; those people either didn't read the book or they weren't paying attention, for Gardner specifically mentions Shakespeare as a moral writer, a playwright who, when dealing with villains like Richard III, or culpable kings like Macbeth, permitted his characters to be complicated and not pushed around by happenstance—not victims—but *actors* in the world. Gardner's premise was that the rules that applied for Sophocles ought still to be applied today.

AV: It seems that critics today are more interested in trying to lump writers into certain camps than they are in paying attention to the rules that applied for Sophocles—however central a concern those rules may be for fiction writers. What is your opinion about artificial groupings such as postmodernism, black humor, historical fiction?

RH: My agent was afraid I would be pigeonholed by doing two novels set in the Old West. That's an occupational hazard, but I didn't let it perturb me. I knew, after all, that I'd written an unpublished contemporary novel and plenty of stories and that my plans were not to stay in the Old West. Any categorization would simply be premature and wrong. Groupings exist for the purpose of newspapers and Ph.D. theses. I know John Barth is supposed to be a postmodernist and John Hawkes a fabulator, but I don't know if these labels can be switched, or where Robert Coover fits into the picture. John Irving, for example, published a novel that was indebted to Gunter Grass, another that brings to mind J.P. Donleavy, a third that continues the stories of Ford Madox Ford and John Hawkes, and so on. The only constant element is John Irving's perspective on these stories—would Grass and Donleavy even speak to one another? And what would Dickens—the writer Irving is most like now—make of the writing of John Hawkes? I'm a great fan of every writer I've mentioned in this interview, and yet I can't think of anything I could say, in general, about all of them except that they're very good writers. Groupings and stereotypings would pit them against each other, and that sort of competition accomplishes nothing at all.

AV: Even so, it seems that all writers are in danger of falling prey to that qualification of their accomplishments. So: twenty—or even thirty—years from now, when you look back at the substantial body of work you've produced, how do you imagine you will have reconciled the tension created by writing what might be termed commercial or "genre" fiction and writing what you yourself have so elegantly referred to as the deepest books in you at the time?

RH: Way too many people approach the writing profession with the same frightened and queasy attitudes fostered by grade school report cards: they're afraid their teachers or peers or reviewers will issue them reprimands for bad deportment. When I published *Desperadoes,* one guy in a creative writing program said he'd been eager to write a Western but didn't think it was okay to do that sort of thing. One of the more peculiar aspects of our creative writing programs is the tendency to "permit" a certain kind of fiction writing while disapproving of many others. It's as if the job of the serious writer were akin to the priesthood of tenth-century monks who could pray in Latin six times a day, but who could neither gossip nor joke.

Entertainment and popular storytelling have become such secondary considerations in creative writing classes that when I mention a story's commercial potential it's frequently seen as a *sub-rosa* rebuke. And yet we writers keep on *reading* books by Isaac Asimov and Elmore Leonard and P.D. James and Stephen King. In my own case, I know that Jules Verne, Edgar Allan Poe, and Robert Louis Stevenson had a great deal to do with my desire to try writing my own stories as a boy, and I would like to make that same impression on someone young or incompletely educated with my own, more accessible books. We unnaturally cripple our intelligence and imagination if, for reasons of pride and narcissism, we deny ourselves the possibility of creating any sort of thing that appeals to us. And any fiction writer who depends on critics or academics for sanction or ratification will end up being insipid, unimportant, and hopelessly mediocre. Writers ought to be instinctive, experimental, perverse, risky, apprehensible. Writing ought to be a natural act, like singing, or a hard kind of play, not a prison of wardens and screws and the jail of "one's career."

AV: *Mariette in Ecstasy* is your third novel. What is it about?

RH: *Mariette in Ecstasy* concerns a seventeen-year-old woman, Mariette Baptiste, who joins the Convent of Our Lady of Sorrows as a postulant in upstate New York in 1906. Her older sister, Annie, or Mother Céline, dies of cancer and is buried. On the next day, Christmas, Mariette is given the stigmata—those wounds in the hands, feet, and side resembling those that Christ suffered on the cross. Whether Mariette is a sexual hysteric full of religious wishful thinking or whether her physical wounds are indeed supernaturally caused is the subject of the novel.

With *Mariette in Ecstasy*, I was not attached to a particular geography or historical period as I was with my previous novels on the Dalton gang and Jesse James. Given that liberty, I roamed freely from France to Nebraska and finally put the convent in upstate New York because I'd taught at Cornell University at Ithaca and was presently teaching at SUNY-Binghamton. I floated through history, too, from the 1700s to 1940, until I finally settled on 1906–1907 because I wanted a historical period far enough in the past that psychoanalysis would just be getting started and medicine would be fairly primitive. I looked for what was necessary for the story, and I did not make historical or technical research harder than it needed to be.

Some parts of the letters Mariette writes in the book, for example, are paraphrased from confessions written by Gemma Galgani in 1900 and included in a hard-to-find book called *Letters and Ecstasies*. Quotidian life in my fictional religious order, the Sisters of the Crucifixion, is based on Thomas Merton's account of the Cistercian life in *The Waters of Siloe*. The mass hysteria hinted at in my book was a product of my looking into Aldous Huxley's wonderful history, *The Devils of Loudun*. Simple scenes of the sisters at work and recreation were inspired by a book of photographs taken at the Carmelite convent in Lisieux by Thérèse's sister Céline. The first investigation of Mariette's stigmata is taken from the medical diagnosis of Padre Pio's stigmata in the 1920s.

I cribbed and stole and adapted from hundreds of sources, finally, but always allowed the factual information to be distorted and transmuted, whether by language or by my own purposeful forgetfulness.

The Forging of Science Fiction

AN INTERVIEW WITH

Greg Bear

G REG B EAR was born on August 20, 1951, in San Diego, California. His father was in the navy, and he spent much of his childhood traveling throughout the Pacific. He wrote his first short story at the age of nine and sold his first story at age fifteen to *Famous Science Fiction*. He graduated from San Diego State University and worked various jobs until he was able to support himself full-time as a writer.

The winner of multiple Nebula and Hugo awards, Bear has published numerous books, including *Beyond Heaven's River* (1980); *Strength of Stones* (1982); *The Wind from a Burning Woman* (1983); *The Infinity Concerto* (1984); *Blood Music* (1985); *Eon* (1985); *The Serpent Maze* (1986); *The Forge of God* (1987); *Eternity* (1988); *Queen of Angels* (1990); *Anvil of Stars* (1992); and *Moving Mars* (1993).

Bear married Astrid Anderson in 1983 and they have a son, Erik, who was born in 1986. They live outside Seattle, in a home that contains a 12,000-book library.

It was science fiction that sparked my interest in reading during high school, though I went on to more serious literature during college. When a friend recommended *Blood Music* by Greg Bear some years later, I realized, after finishing the book, that I had been away from science fiction too long. I contacted Greg Bear about doing an interview in 1988, but we were unable to get together until March 17, 1989, when he came to Houston to sign copies of his novel *Eternity* at Future Visions bookstore. The interview was conducted between booksignings in a room at a Motel 6 on the outskirts of Houston. We sat across from each other at a small, round formica table and were only interrupted by a few incoming phone calls.

Greg Bear looks like a working-class guy, but during the course of the interview, he proved to be a man of keen intellect as well as an opinionated bookworm. He has read most of the 12,000 books in his home library, and his range of knowledge is impressive: physics, xeniobiology, history, astronomy, literature. He discussed these subjects as though they exist in a database he can tap into in order to imagine the various possible futures that await us in an ever-changing universe.

AV: Since you are a graduate of San Diego State University, how did you develop an interest in science fiction when most college classes are geared toward conventional literature?

GB: I was a big science fiction fan long before I went to college. I was interested in science fiction by the time I was eight or nine years old. I sold my first story in high school.

AV: What was your attitude toward the standard English classes?

GB: They were fine. If the teachers were good, I enjoyed them. I'm a very diverse reader. I don't have any particular prejudices.

AV: Your books contain references and allusions to various writers. For example, *The Infinity Concerto* acknowledgment mentions Jorge Luis Borges, while *Eon* and *Eternity* character Konrad Korzenowski is the actual Polish name of Joseph Conrad. Just as Borges has stated that "writers create their own precursors," can you mention the writers that influenced you?

GB: I'll start with the science fiction writers first. The usual gang of suspects: Robert Heinlein, Arthur C. Clarke, Isaac Asimov, and Ray Bradbury probably influenced me the most. Bradbury, in particular, because I knew him personally. He was a direct model of what a writer did and could be. I started corresponding with Ray when I was about sixteen and continue to this day. So he has been a very big influence. Arthur C. Clarke, of all the living science fiction writers, is probably the most influential on the kind of stories that I write, that I think are what science fiction should be. He concerns himself with both science and philosophy at the same time. He's a true visionary.

AV: What about Kurt Vonnegut?

GB: Vonnegut is a fine writer, but he came to my attention after my formative period. *Slaughter-House Five*, I think, is a masterpiece. Outside of American pulp science fiction, Olaf Stapledon has had the most influence on me. His works inspired Arthur C. Clarke. After seeing *2001*, I traced Clarke's roots back to Stapledon. *Last and First Men* and *Starmaker* were very formative. Then, of course, the oldtimers, like H. G. Wells, had an enormous impact on me as a child and teenager. Wells and Verne, Asimov and Clarke, and Bradbury and Heinlein all built the bedrock; Stapledon and other writers laid on the superstructure.

Outside of science fiction completely, I enjoy reading James Joyce, Joseph Conrad, and, in my college years, Nikos Kazantzakis. I found a resonance between the philosophies of Kazantzakis and Stapledon. Later, I found a similar vein in Bradbury's work; Bradbury was very fond of Kazantzakis' "Spiritual Exercises." Jorge Luis Borges I discovered about the same time as Kazantzakis. *Other Inquisitions* was the collection of Borges' essays that I read first. I enjoyed it immensely. Borges was a literary writer not in the least afraid of ideas. He reveled in them. What he was afraid of was long narrative—he thought it was unnecessary. Yet he adored Cervantes.

AV: Borges also has an element of science fiction in his works.

GB: He read a lot of science fiction. I met him when he was lecturing at San Diego State in about 1970. I came up after his talk and managed to get one of his books autographed. He was nearly blind, and the autograph is a seismograph scrawl. "You mentioned H. P. Lovecraft," I said. "How much of Lovecraft have you actually read?" Borges replied, "I've read a little bit of him. But Lovecraft—that's a wonderful name for a writer—don't you think?" And he laughed. Of course, Borges had read Bradbury and A. E. Van Vogt—he talks about them in his essays on American literature. An absolutely unprejudiced man. Maybe he was prejudiced about Argentine literature, but he looked at English and American literature as a vast foreign thing which he had to absorb, and he valued English and American fantasy and science fiction for the wealth of ideas.

AV: I recall in some of his interviews that Borges said American writers had the greatest impact on him. This was probably because his father had a sizable library that contained a lot of American literature.

GB: I think we all love most what we start reading in our teenage years.

AV: You also mention Anthony Burgess in "The Wind From A Burning Woman," where one of the characters in the story was reading Burgess.

GB: Yes, and I've neglected to mention James Blish, who wrote several novels that were very influential on me. Chiefly, *Black Easter* and *A Case of Conscience*, but also books like *Jack of Eagles*. He had wonderful science fiction ideas. He also came up with some philosophical ideas that were really quite startling even if he didn't develop them fully. In *Black Easter* he talked briefly about radiation destroying the physical soul. That really stuck with me, and it turned into *Psychlone*, which is in part dedicated to him. In *A Case of Conscience*, Blish referred to *Finnegans Wake* by James Joyce. So I immediately hustled off and bought a copy and became a real Joyce fanatic. I still appreciate *Finnegans Wake* more than *Ulysses*. I started with the most difficult book of all.

AV: Borges has also referred to the library as a universe. I understand you are a voracious reader in a variety of fields, which has resulted in the collection of over twelve thousand books in your own library at your house in Washington. What is your daily reading and writing schedule like?

GB: If you count books by weight, my library came to seventeen thousand pounds when we moved about two years ago. As far as my reading habits, I read in the bathtub, I read before going to bed at night and, if I'm doing research on something, I'll be reading in the daytime.

My writing schedule is not really fixed. I write each day until I've amassed five pages, but I don't stop myself if I'm really rolling. I seldom reach ten pages a day because I start getting ahead of myself if I do. The plotting has to go on in the background.

AV: How did you make that transition after you graduated from college to be a self-supporting writer? I think at one time you worked in a bookstore.

GB: That's almost all I did. Actually, my first wife, Tina, helped a lot because she was gainfully employed. I was able to repay her in part by giving her a year off later on. Astrid was also gainfully employed. She only got off work three years ago, which was just before our son was born. She hasn't worked since because we are doing quite well. Mostly it's been a matter of working very, very hard and having the support of a spouse.

AV: How did you work in those days? Did you work full time in the bookstore for forty hours a week and write at night?

GB: It was sporadic because I was going to school. By 1975 I was free-lancing full time. Before that I was going to school and working part time or full time in the Space Theatre in San Diego. I had different odd jobs, but no sense of a career other than being a writer.

AV: Do you feel there is less pressure to write such as when you had a job, or is there more pressure to write when writing is a full-time profession?

GB: You can call it pressure, but I think it's more *internal* pressure since you don't have someone leaning over you. I found very early that I could work with people who I knew were as smart or smarter than I am, but I had a really difficult time working with people who were dumber and that's what you have to do in the workaday world as a general rule. You quite often have to get along with people who are less intelligent.

AV: Something like the Peter Principle. You run into those people on the way up.

GB: I'm fortunate since publishers are never dumb; at least my publishers aren't! I really don't have to worry about them. I really don't have any bosses. I just have people who are happy if I'm getting the work done on time.

AV: To quote from the preface of *The Wind from a Burning Woman:* "The future will come, and it will be different, unimaginably so." And to quote a line by Kawashita from *Beyond Heaven's River:* "The future is not appetizing." Would you concur that this is an ongoing theme in your books—that the future for mankind is ever-changing and not necessarily pleasant and predictable? Or, to be more precise, that Heisenberg's Uncertainty Principle is a scientific metaphor in your books?

GB: As far as the future being unimaginable, yes. Human beings are a chaotic system. Certainly, history reflects a chaotic system, which means you cannot predict how humans are going to behave over the long term. You might be able to do gross analogies by characterizing our role in a biological system. You might say that at this point, if human beings belong to a giant biological system on the Earth, they are equivalent to the Earth's gonads.

Perhaps cultures will grow old and stagnant and will be replaced by new cultures. There is no way beyond that generalization to pin down what might happen.

AV: And that's probably good, in one sense.

GB: It's wonderful in one sense, and it's horrible in another sense. If you think history should be a lot of people having a very good time and not being in any great pain, history is not like that. History is a very, very nasty, prolonged, painful adolescence right now. The twentieth century is the bloodiest century we have ever been through—and it continues to be. We have seen so-called developed people who, at the same time as seeming to be fairly reasonable and rational people, are capable of doing the most nasty, mean, rotten things. And yet if you met them on the street, they would be fairly good party guests.

AV: Are you referring to people like Hitler or Stalin?

GB: Hitler or Stalin probably would not have been very good at a party. Hitler got into power because Germany was twisted by WWI and its aftermath. Germany was just basically ground under and stomped on by all the European nations, whereupon it went crazy. Germany expressed its craziness in an urge to suicide, which is particularly Germanic. They picked Hitler to lead them to the funeral parlor.

AV: What about the Japanese?

GB: The Japanese are a different problem. The Japanese came out of the feudal period into the twentieth century in a period of about forty years. By 1900 they had battleships and they had all the modern war machines that all the other nations had. They had already whipped the Chinese and the Russians by the time the nation had been out of the feudal period only forty-five years. So you might think of Japan as coming out of childhood and going immediately into late adolescence and having to catch up with everybody else, yet still living by a philosophy and creed of a society that was back in the feudal period. They had to shake that loose, and, unfortunately, they had to shake it loose in the middle of all this other stuff. They got very badly burned. Interestingly enough, they recovered from World War II with the help of the United States. The Marshall Plan was unheard of in the history of warfare. Nearly every nation that we defeated came out stronger than they were before the war. Japan certainly did so although the U.S. can't take all the credit for that. There is an innate genius in Japan. It perhaps even transcends the innate genius that you still find in Germany. A lot of their problems had to do with major cultural difficulties. For example, Germany did not become a unified country until the nineteenth century. It never had a sense of a unified culture. The U.S. had to acquire that in the Civil War. Before that time, each part of the U.S. thought of itself as a separate nation. We still have those tendencies. You know, the Pacific Northwest thinks it's far better than California. California is despised by New York. And New York is loathed by everybody else. All these schisms exist.

AV: In your novel *Eternity,* the Recovery reminded me of the Marshall Plan. The Hexamon group tried to help the native Earthlings recover economically and psychologically to the level where they were before the battle with the Jarts.

GB: It's a good comparison, although we were not at war with the Hexamon. They had a chance to redeem their past. For example, try to imagine someone going back after WWI and teaching Europe how to organize to avoid the next forty years of misery and to avoid a Europe and a Russia driven crazy by deprivation and war.

Almost every problem we have now in the Western world comes out of that period. It comes out of the decision after WWI to start grinding nations down. The

Depression perhaps came out of that. Winston Churchill thought so. It seems a good theory to me because there was so much bad money being pumped out of Germany to pay off war debts that they couldn't possibly repay. Russia got caught up in a revolution that was misdirected because of WWI. You wonder what would have happened if some decent, reasonable men had been in place instead of some of the massive incompetents that were in charge of Europe at that time. After WWI, there were decent men with ideas of how history operated. Men like George C. Marshall and MacArthur in Japan. For a conquering war hero, MacArthur was an amazingly sophisticated social worker.

AV: He was more of a diplomat than a soldier after the war.

GB: He was far more important to the world as a diplomat than as a soldier, and these things are to America's credit. I hope the future looks back on us for that reason and not for the things we screwed up. In other areas, we screwed up horribly—for example, in the occupations of Central America and Haiti. Even today we continue to screw up in these countries. We just don't know what to be: a strong-arm world police force or a benevolent world helper.

AV: There also seem to be a number of characters and ideas that grow into a more full-bodied development. I'm referring to such short stories as "The Wind from a Burning Woman" *(Eon* and *Eternity),* "Mandala" *(Strength of Stones),* and "Blood Music" *(Blood Music).* Can you explain how this happens?

GB: Some ideas develop a life of their own. There's a tradition in science fiction that if your book takes off like a rocket, then you write a sequel to it. In most of these cases, the stories didn't take off like rockets, although "Blood Music" did very well. I was actually planning the novel before "Blood Music" won any awards. The idea contained in the story was not fully developed in the short version. It was there, it was nicely handled, it came to a striking conclusion, it got its point across; but there were a lot of other implications that had to be developed, so I wrote a book.

AV: What about "The Wind from a Burning Woman," written around 1976, which was a prelude to *Eon* that came out in 1984?

GB: I started writing *Eon* about 1979. I think "The Wind from a Burning Woman" was fairly well developed as a story, but it had an interesting culture in it that posed some curious problems. I think it was Orson Scott Card who reviewed the story and said it was an interesting story but that he couldn't believe that society could have ever existed. Of course, there was no history in the novel-ette. So I went back and filled in the history and stuck it into *Eon* as a support for this big idea of this infinite artificial universe.

AV: *Blood Music* was one of the most distinctive science fiction novels in recent years. How did this novel develop, particularly your knowledge of genetics?

GB: To write the short story, I had to do just a little bit of research. It was short enough that I could get by with just a few references. To do the novel, I had to go out and really add to what I knew about genetics—which was very little. I have a pretty good background in astronomy and physics, less in biology and genetics. I've been around enough scientists to pick up their jargon and know their personalities. What I really had to do was go out and visit biology laboratories where people were working that were like my people in the story. I did that by making appointments with several professors at the University of California at San Diego and the Scripps Institute of Oceanography. I found several young people, who are mentioned in the back of the book, who were very sympathetic to my work. They were all professors or researchers at the university or at the Institute. So they went to work in the labs while I sat watching them and their techniques, noting the types of equipment they worked with, and using the Stephen King technique of putting in brand names if you can because it makes a story more authentic.

AV: What about Vergil I. Ulam's name? I assume it's an anagram or that "I.V." could stand for "intravenous."

GB: Oh, it's much simpler than that. For one thing, Ulam is a good Polish name. It's a real name, but it's also an anagram. You will have to work out the anagram. Switch around the letters, and it spells out the name of a well-known literary character who was also involved with the very small.

AV: Please discuss the idea of the Thought Universe and its ongoing dialogue with Dr. Bernard, which is an interesting concept in *Blood Music*.

GB: I'm not sure who first came up with the notion behind Thought Universe. If we go back far enough, we get some hints of it in Alfred Bester's *The Stars My Destination*. I think the first author to really write about it in detail was John Varley, but I could be wrong. Someone like Fred Pohl or Jack Williamson is sure to have done it at some point in time. William Hjortsborg used it to some extent in a book called *Grey Matters*. John Varley wrote stories like "Overdrawn at the Memory Bank," where he talks about the computer being a receptacle for the human spirit. We must not leave out *Neuromancer* by William Gibson, who invented the term "cyber-space." Cyberspace may be a better name for what we're talking about than Thought Universe—it's certainly caught the public imagination and will likely end up in the dictionary—but I think Thought Universe is more descriptive.

The possibility occurred to me when I was doing research on an article on computer graphics that if you could simply move computer graphics into the human brain or the brain into the computer, as in *Tron*, then you've got a simulation of existence for the actual soul or spirit or programming, or whatever you want to call it, that is the equivalent of reality. And that's a huge metaphor for life itself. You can think of the entire universe as nothing but information running back and forth. So a Thought Universe then becomes a less rigorously controlled metaphor for the universe.

AV: Many readers might see the end of *Blood Music* and the end of humanity, as we know it, as disquieting. Yet I think you were trying to convey that this change to a different life form is just another example of evolution. Is this a correct analysis? Also, you made a point earlier about the whole earth having a consciousness as a collective biological system. Does this analogy apply here?

GB: I'm not a complete believer in James Lovelock's theory of Gaia—the Living Earth. I don't think the Living Earth is a conscious entity, and I don't think you can say it's a biological organism like a human being. To compare them would be like comparing a human being to a cell. A human being is an entirely different structure from a cell. Gaia would be a completely different structure from a human being. For example, it might not have parents. A planet is very likely to be self-generating.

There is natural evolution, and there is man's evolution. Most evolution is blind. It doesn't have soft sensibilities about cuddly, furry animals. Many millions of deaths or trillions of deaths have to occur for an evolutionary process to take place.

AV: At least until this century. We may have a say in what may or may not be here.

GB: Right now, natural evolution is not the only path to large-scale change. We are now in the process of controlling evolution as a *means to our own ends*. I suspect we will be surprised. I wrote a metaphor about how we might be surprised. Turning into lime jello is a pretty surprising way to evolve! Especially when you find out it's wonderful.

AV: You think that would be wonderful? What do you think would be the pros and cons of this type of evolution?

GB: Well, very few people actually died in *Blood Music*. The whole world is gone as far as we know it, and the whole structure is different, but if you look at the last chapter, one of the characters (Bernard) goes back and is able to correct the mistakes of his youth in a simulation.

AV: Yes, but it's only thought. It's like a dream with no physical contact.

GB: But you wouldn't know the difference. Remember—they're fully sensory. They're disembodied spirits provided with a completely simulated environment. For example, right now you could be in Thought Universe, but you wouldn't know it. Maybe it's already happened, and we're just sitting here discussing it, and this is an artistic jape on behalf of the noocytes. You wouldn't know the difference so long as you were in that simulated environment. It's a bit of a conundrum, of course.

AV: So you are saying that if Bernard and the girl he missed having as the love of his life had been reunited at an earlier age, and that if they had had intercourse, then it would have been the same as having real physical intercourse?

GB: Yes, they could simulate the entire existence of that other life and then they could go off and try marriage. In other words, they experience a kind of heavenly immortality, unbounded in space and time unless they choose it.

AV: Wouldn't this be restricted to the past and not to the future?

GB: In Thought Universe you can simulate anything. You can change the rules of the game, including metaphysical rules. You can tweak Euclid's fifth postulate and end up with unimaginable varieties of experiences that you simply cannot do within the limited context of our physical universe.

AV: What about exploring outer space from the Thought Universe?

GB: Outer space is *within* you. Look what happened at the end. Everything, including the planets, is sucked in. The universe has been attacked from the bottom level, from the level of all smallness in creation and reconstructed as thought and information. Space exploration is unnecessary if all of space and time are contained within your universe. You have basically digested the entire world all at once.

AV: *The Forge of God* is an apocalyptic novel that delves into such topics as politics and religion. Please discuss the exchange in which Crockerman asks, "Do you believe in God?" and the Guest replies, "We believe in punishment."

GB: The Guest was playing with the President's head. But the Guest itself is just a tool of the machine intelligence that is already dissolving the planet. The Guest is just sitting there going boogey-boogey—saying, I know you are a lowly human being, we know how to mess with your mind, and we're curious what happens when we do.

AV: I thought the Guest was just a parasite.

GB: That's only what it claimed to be! It was lying. And so were the robots who were saying "Welcome to the galactic culture." It becomes pretty obvious to the characters later on in the book that they're being tested like ants in a nest, having a stick poked at them by "intellects vast and cool and unsympathetic." The intellects already know basically what the human reactions are going to be. They know how to prod this low-level culture. You hit these particular buttons. Most humans are in a particular religious phase, and the President is the leader of a fairly religious society. The machine invaders know religion as we could not possibly know it—complete from outside, seeing it as a morphological phenomenon. It's like observing hormone flows inside the human body. They know how religion works. They take a look at us and say, "We can poke them here and see what happens, and we'll run our experiment before we destroy the Earth."

The robot probes have three functions. One is to reproduce themselves. Two is to destroy species that could compete with their original masters. Three is to study everything they get their hands on. Everything the killer probes do in *The Forge of God* is explained by these three provisions. There are also machine intelligences opposed to the planet-killing probes. They arrive when the humans are completely confused. (It's possible the reader will be confused for a while as well.) They have different motives. They consider it a gross breach of galactic law to create self-replicating machines that go off and do your dirty work for you.

AV: I read a review of *The Forge of God* by a critic who said that by having the bogus spaceships, you had cheated the reader by "injecting false suspense into the narrative."

GB: My reply to the critic is, "Do your homework! Slow down. Read the book carefully." There are whole chapters in the novel that answer his criticism in plain text and not hidden away in some obscure metaphor.

AV: What about *The Forge of God* being an apocalyptic novel? Many people have the idea that if there are beings out there of higher intelligence, they must therefore be good, but you seem to be saying that isn't necessarily the case.

GB: A long time ago, David Brin and I were talking about a galactic ecology. He was trying to find an explanation why Von Neumann probes hadn't filled the entire galaxy. If you had one civilization develop efficient Von Neumann probes, then in 100,000 years they would suck up virtually the entire galaxy.

It occurred to me that you don't have straightforward developments in any natural system. For example, on Earth we have many biological systems—species—competing with other species. One system develops here, another system develops there, and if they're going to fight for the same territory then they start fighting each other. That spurs evolution. It spurs change. It also creates a dynamic stasis, dynamic interaction where one gives and the other takes.

Occasionally one will dominate completely, and then it will weaken or fall prey and another will take its niche. It's an evolutionary process. So why not extend that to the entire galaxy? This critic, as so often happens with critics, is just not thinking broadly enough. He hasn't broken out of the old mind set. He thinks, "Oh, gee, he's talking about God here." No, I'm not talking about God. The machines are using God to torment the poor President of the United States. They don't give a damn about God! In this novel, God has nothing to say about what the killer probes are doing. God is far removed from the discussion of this novel—if He exists at all. In *Eternity,* I talked about God. I mean, there is a vision of God, if you want one, coming to save us. God is ourselves, but infinitely older.

AV: Are you referring to "The Final Mind," or the "Descendant Command," as the Jarts called them?

GB: Yes. I have religious elements in many of my books, but they can't be understood in the standard fashion.

AV: What about your fellow writers? Do they understand and respond to your writing better than the critics?

GB: I haven't received too many bad comments from fellow writers. Books are funny that way. You'll find some writers are really opposed to some books. One writer didn't like *Eon* very much at all. He thought it was too metaphysical and too undisciplined, but he absolutely loved *The Forge of God.* He just keyed in on everything that happened in it. In some respects, he's right. *The Forge of God* is a better formal novel than *Eon.* It was written a few years later. Hopefully, I'm getting better.

I'm taking themes that involve strong human emotions, and expand them to a large scale. *The Forge of God* is a book about the death of friends—up to and including the death of the Earth.

One of the characters (Harry Feinman) has cancer. His cancer serves as a microcosm of the Earth, which also has a cancer. The kid, Rueben Bordes, has just lost his mother, and it has not only torn up his family, but it is going to happen to Rueben again when the Earth is destroyed. It's not apparent to most readers what's going on here, but it should echo subconsciously in their heads. When you re-emphasize the story from several different angles then the story becomes triply strong. That's what I love doing. I've just finished a book called *Queen of Angels*, which spins a story through several viewpoints, reflecting at least five strongly echoing themes.

AV: It seems there has always been an unholy war between art and religion as well as between science and religion; yet, *The Forge of God* seems to walk the middle ground. What are your thoughts about religion in contemporary society?

GB: I think it is more science versus religion. Religion has always managed to subvert art to its own purpose, and then art sneaks around and subverts religion. But science is a more direct, cantankerous individual, and, consequently, science and religion have usually squared off pretty drastically.

AV: It's going on right now, with the Creationists trying to influence the content of the textbooks used in high schools.

GB: The Creationists want to go back three thousand or four thousand years and have a static society that has never existed on this Earth. They want to force it on everybody. I've got one thing to say to them: "You can go live in Iran and have a good time. It's not going to happen here."

AV: When asked if he was an atheist, Woody Allen's character in *Annie Hall* responded that he considered himself "part of God's loyal opposition." What is your notion about God?

GB: If God were any sort of decent God at all he would certainly have a loyal opposition. I spend most of my life not telling God what to be. I certainly haven't the slightest clue as to what a God should be. So I keep playing at describing what a God could be, but I'm not going to be dogmatic about it. It's ridiculous. I'm not equipped. None of us is intellectually equipped to handle the concept of a God. It's a toy for our own development.

AV: What about the role of Crockerman and his use of religion as a crutch?

GB: Crockerman is not a political statement about any particular party. Crockerman is a very good politician. He's the kind of politician we find commonly in the United States today. He's just not an intellectual politician. He can't handle big, philosophical problems. Yet, suddenly, he's got one laid in his lap. He strives for a solution that allows him to continue to be a good leader. Obviously his religious background is such that he believes in some deep sense that the Apocalypse is at hand. And he asks us to prepare for it.

AV: Both *Eon* and *Eternity,* your latest novel, offer some fascinating ideas about the future of mankind. How did you develop the concept for these books, especially about the Stone and the Way?

GB: The seven chambers of the hollowed-out asteroid come from the story "The Wind from a Burning Woman." After the asteroid has been flying around for five hundred years or so, the people inside get very tired of waiting to arrive at their star system. You have the equivalent of millions and millions of people inside this thing. They create this artificial universe using the physics that had been pioneered even before the end of the twentieth century by people like Patricia Vasquez. They look back upon her as a pioneer. It's more than a literary twist of fate that she shows up on board the Stone and gets to meet Korzenowski. This is stretching the filaments of history considerably, but it's fun. She gets to meet all the people for whom she was the godmother.

The last chapter of *Eon* is given considerably more detail in *Eternity*. We explore the alternate universe that she fell into rather than getting back home where she wanted to be.

AV: Can you briefly discuss the role of the Jarts (originally described in *Eon* as monstrously aggressive fleas), which seem to be somewhat analogous to Milton's satanic angel in *Paradise Lost*?

GB: I suppose that's not a bad comparison. The Jarts are alien and domineering and as advanced physically and technologically as the Hexamon. You're never quite sure what they were, originally, because they have shape-changed so much. They can be whatever they want to be.

The original Jart figure that we see locked in stasis was identified by a reader who wrote a letter to me and asked, "Is this based on the Cambrian creature found in the Burgess shales (*Hallucigenia Sparsa*)?" Well, damn right it is! That's one of my favorite creatures—this little spiked thing running around in the Cambrian period. The kid read it and recognized it. That's great. Kids are my best critics sometimes.

AV: Your next novel is *Queen of Angels*. What can we look forward to in this book?

GB: I just finished it recently. I'm probably too close to it right now to say, but it's probably the best thing that I have ever written. It's a near-future novel—comparable to *Stand On Zanzibar* or *Brave New World*. It has to do with self-awareness and punishment as well as our society's preoccupation with both of those things and the really weird mix of the two. As far as I can tell right now, it works better than any novel I've written. Virtually everything ties together and echoes the central themes.

AV: When will it be out?

GB: Probably early next year, around January of 1990.

AV: What do you mean when you say our society is preoccupied with punishment?

GB: If someone came along and murdered your daughter, would you sit down and recommend psychological therapy for him, or would you want to put him in an endless hell?

AV: Endless hell, of course!

GB: You see, you're preoccupied with punishment. We don't care so much about other people so much as we want them to either leave us alone or face eternal damnation. We see it throughout human cultures. Poor Salman Rushdie. What are they going to do with him? They're going to send him straight to hell because he offended their sensibilities. Well, it's pretty obvious that Salman Rushdie didn't offend Allah one bit—I don't see Allah pinning him down with a thunderbolt! Allah sends his little children out to do the dirty work, I guess.

AV: It helps to get the dirty work done when there's a five million dollar fee on Rushdie's head.

GB: This kind of nonsense extends into our culture. I'm not immune to this. I'm just as glad that Ted Bundy is no longer with us. On the other hand, would I have put Ted Bundy in eternal hell? Would I put Hitler in eternal hell? Of all people, you wonder about Hitler or some of the tyrants of the twentieth century, like Stalin or Mao, who put so many countless millions of people through unbelievable misery—what should their fates be? Very likely, in nature, they're just dead. And that's going to happen to me, too, and I haven't done anything nearly as evil. So that's not fair. Society's answer is to punish the bastards! In the society of *Queen of Angels* it is possible to do so.

So, in *Queen of Angels* not only is the potential for really nasty punishment there, but the potential as well for therapy, in the sense of taking a person who has done a horrible thing and finding out what's wrong with him. And then correcting him without removing his personality or substantially affecting him as a self-aware individual.

AV: From where does the title derive?

GB: You'll have to read the book to find that out. It's pretty deeply embedded and has at least three meanings.

AV: If therapy ever reaches the stage of curing the evil that men do, then aren't you putting us in the position of a god?

GB: We are beginning to understand more and more about human personality and how the brain works. It's almost inevitable that there will come a time when effective psychological therapy will exist. Right now it's all just magic and smoke and occasional miracle cures. We are like children in dealing with our own brains because we don't know what's going on in them. But there will come a time when we will. This book has to address all those questions.

We are a lot more civilized than we used to be. I think we are in a transition state. We are growing toward a time when we don't want revenge so much as we want to cure people who behave in evil and destructive ways. We see their behavior as a disease.

AV: If we can correct these people, then are we turning mankind into a kind of robot?

GB: Good question, isn't it? What's the difference between Ted Bundy and you and I? He's the robot. He's the one who is stuck on one particular, very nasty habit. Here's Ted Bundy telling us all about pornography. How pornography sent him off in this direction. There are millions upon millions of young American males out there who read the same things Bundy did and they didn't turn into mass murderers. What is Bundy? He is a monster. An aberration. He's like a giant cancer. If you can cure his robotic behavior, give him back self-control, does that turn you into a robot maker?

AV: Hopefully, more of a doctor.

GB: Exactly. You are curing this illness, this aberration that he has. There is a question that occurs in *Queen of Angels*: What if you find out that the root of evil is the root of a personality? Then, as a social worker, do we have the right to expunge the personality and put in a new one?

AV: There is a project going on at Jet Propulsion Laboratory (JPL) whereby a spacecraft would measure the distances between stars, thereby revealing if the universe is expanding or contracting. What are your thoughts on these two polar (universal life versus entropic death) possibilities?

GB: It's expanding. It's pretty obvious. We just don't know how it's expanding or how fast or how long it will go.

AV: Do you think it will ever collapse?

GB: It's possible. We just don't know. We don't have solid answers yet. I tend to like the notion of a cyclical universe. On the other hand the options may be unknown.

AV: With science fiction writers such as Benford, Brin, Card, Gibson, Leguin, yourself, and others, science fiction seems to be coming closer to literature. Do you like the thought that science fiction is being considered as "serious literature," or would you prefer it to maintain its own separate genre?

GB: It's there. We're not coming close. We're better than most of the writers writing today because we handle important questions like "Whither mankind?"

I think someone quoted Barth as saying, "Science fiction writers are not like you and I. They have more fun!" That's a wonderful quote. And it's true! You get a bunch of serious literary writers together, and they're good company because they're intelligent. But then you put them in a room with a couple of freaks like me or Brin or Benford, and we're going to be running all up and down the spectrum. We're going to switch from hard physics and xenobiology to the course of Moslem history in the twentieth century. What are they stuck with? They're stuck with the past or the twentieth century. Most know nothing about science or physics or astronomy.

Now with some of them, this is not true. Pynchon is apparently able to swim in these waters pretty well. John Updike is an extremely bright man who has written science fiction–like stories and fantasy stories. *Witches of Eastwick* is an out-and-out horror-fantasy story with sexual overtones.

So the really good writers aren't prejudiced in what they address. Unfortunately, there are too many writers who are wallflowers at the orgy. Science fiction writers are definitely not wallflowers at the orgy. They *are* the orgy! They're a vast wellspring of ideas and to see them at work is amazing.

Other writers can go off and pontificate, and we'll see whose name is remembered four hundred years from now. That's the challenge. It's probably not going to be mine, and we will all be equal under the grave—but at least I will have laid down that challenge.

AV: Finally, is the name Vergil I. Ulam an anagram for Gulliver?

GB: Close. It translates to "I am Gulliver."

A Life of Perished Things

AN INTERVIEW WITH

Marilynne Robinson

M ARILYNNE R OBINSON was born in 1944 and raised in northern Idaho, where her family has lived for several generations. She graduated from Brown University in 1966, where she studied writing with John Hawkes, and she received her Ph.D. in American literature in 1977 from the University of Washington.

Housekeeping was published in 1982 when she was thirty-eight. It was nominated for the Pulitzer Prize, won the Hemingway Foundation Award for Best First Novel, and later was made into a feature movie. *Mother Country* was published in 1988 and was a finalist for the National Book Award in nonfiction.

The interview was conducted by phone on March 15, 1993. She spoke to me from her office at the University of Iowa, where she teaches at the Writers' Workshop. Throughout the interview her voice was mirthful and her laughter engaging. Not only did she convey a vast understanding of the process of writing, but was incredibly well versed on a range of subjects from history to contemporary social and environmental issues.

AV: Do you look upon the writing of fiction as a way to exorcize pain, to give memory some type of permanence, or something else altogether?

MR: Something else altogether. I've always had trouble

describing to people what I think fiction actually is, but I think it's not more securely anchored in biographical or psychological experiences than something like a painting or sculpture would be. I think of fictions as freestanding objects that exist for their own value. I really hesitate to say I have written or would write fiction to satisfy some other purpose other than simply my interest in writing fiction.

AV: You mentioned in an interview with Kay Bonetti [Audio Prose Library] that while you were working on your dissertation a professor said he would like to see some of your fiction. Since there was nothing from your undergraduate days you wanted to show him, you went to the library and fell asleep. Then you woke up and proceeded to write that whole passage in *Housekeeping* about the grandfather who subsequently dies when the train plummets into Fingerbone Lake. This passage seems to have been the germ for the whole novel—yet it's almost like you dreamed it. What are your recollections of this fantastic story within a story?

MR: It's actually fairly much as you described it. I had this story in mind more or less whole that day in the library. I don't know why. I didn't, at that point, think of it as part of a novel. I think it was related to many other things that preoccupied me at that time. It seems like it was something I was simply inventing out of whole cloth for perfectly accidental reasons; and yet there it was. I do remember I was very engaged by the writing of it when it occurred.

AV: You studied creative writing at Brown University with John Hawkes as your teacher. What was this experience like, and did Hawkes influence your writing style?

MR: John Hawkes was a wonderful editor of my writing. He made me aware very quickly of when I was writing well and when I was not writing well. It helped to sensitize me very effectively, I think, to what the possibilities of my writing style were. He didn't allude to his own writing when he taught. So the similarities some people find between our styles were more the consequence of his teaching influence bonding to my writing than my looking at his.

AV: What writers influenced you, and which ones do you admire?

MR: I suppose I have been influenced by practically everything I've read. The writers I most consciously respond to are the nineteenth-century American writers like Melville, Dickinson, Poe, and Twain. I've always found that to be a very rich period, but it seems to me it ended before it was completed in a way. I was very interested in taking up what seemed to be philosophical or theosophical or aesthetic issues which they brought up, but too few people carried forward. I have also been influenced by such writers as Wallace Stevens and William Faulkner.

AV: You said the nineteenth century ended before it was completed, but aren't writers like you still carrying on that tradition? It seems writers like you or Ron Hansen or Kazus Ishiguro are writing more in the vein of nineteenth-century or early twentieth-century stylists rather than that of the more contemporary twentieth-century writers or even the twenty-first century, which looms around the corner.

MR: I think it takes a lot of looking backward to decide which is the real style of the twenty-first or the twentieth century. I think people like Hemingway are very much descendants of the kind of writing that interests me. Also, I think people feel some nervous obligation to come up with what they take to be a contemporary style, but whether it lasts or amounts to anything is another question.

AV: You stated in the interview with Bonetti that while "working on my dissertation I began to feel as though I had lost the option of being a fiction writer." Why? Was there something about being in that ivory tower of academic research that made you feel more an observer than a participant?

MR: I never experienced it as an ivory tower. I feel I'm much more in an ivory tower when I'm writing fiction, as a matter of fact. The prevailing wisdom of the time was that you do one thing or you do the other. I think it has been fairly unusual for people to get academic Ph.D.s and to write fiction. The idea was, if you develop one style of writing or one habit of mind, then it more or less precluded the other.

AV: You said in an interview with the *Iowa Review* that "I've probably thought of Poe at least once a day every day since I was ten years old. I've never quite understood this incredible affinity. It's probably unhealthy." Aunt Sylvie in *Housekeeping* can be viewed as an extension of the lonely, morbid world of Poe, but how do you see your writing style compared with Poe's? For example, *Housekeeping* explores that dark and lonely world, but the spiritual tone of the book is positive and optimistic compared with Poe.

MR: As I said when I was talking to Kay Bonetti, I don't really understand my affinity with Poe. One thing I see in Poe is a very deep intelligence. His prose is very elegant and carefully wrought. I think Poe is a philosophic writer. It's hard to explain precisely what I mean by that, because I've spent a lot of time trying to explain it to myself. If you read his essay "Eureka," you can see how his mind is working and how seriously he undertakes prose.

I don't think of Sylvie as morbid at all. I wouldn't ever use that word to characterize her. I don't think of Poe as being as nearly as morbid or pessimistic as everyone thinks. I don't even think "pessimism" is exactly the word that I would apply to Poe. One of the things that struck me about Poe when I was young was that he was probably the only writer in literature who admired women for being good at mathematics. The things he found attractive and fascinating were the mastery of obscure languages and things that were somewhat esoteric. And in the oddest way, I think it was a liberating idea for me when I was a young girl.

AV: You said that "Poe really feels as though he's writing to himself." Do you think this holds true for you and other serious writers?

MR: I think to the degree writers are serious there is a greater tendency for them to write to themselves, because they are trying to compose their own thoughts. They are trying to find out what is in their minds, which is the great mystery. Finding out who you are, what is in your head, and what kind of companion you are to yourself in the course of life. One of the things that is interesting about writing is that it does give you some access to that, and it's quite surprising to find what's there.

AV: You also mention that the characteristic mode of thought of most classic American writers is "based on the assumption that the only way to understand the world is metaphorical, and all metaphors are inadequate, and that you press them far enough and you're delivered into something that requires a new articulation." Can you elaborate on this, since you certainly make use of metaphors, and could you also clarify the meaning of a "new articulation"?

MR: I think, to a certain extent, what I mean is a new metaphor or a larger or a more refined metaphor. Also to the extent that the system is working well for you or the method is working for you, you are discovering things that are authentic discoveries rather than repeating or rephrasing things you have acquired out of other people's thinking. It bears a very strong comparison with the methods of speculative science. It bears a strong comparison with almost any kind of ambitious thinking that people do. The important thing for me is that metaphor is not ornamental; it's methodological. It has something to do with the way in which truth is inaccessible and the way in which truth is also accessible. That is the means by which in its own highly bracketed and conditional way it is accessible.

AV: You once stated that "I don't think I could have written *Housekeeping* if I hadn't had children." Why? Is there a connection beteeen your children and the characters in the novel?

MR: No. I just wouldn't have known all the sorts of strange emotional dynamics of having your identity invested in another person. I wouldn't have known the disparity between how you perceive yourself and how you are perceived by people that are very dear to you.

AV: You have also said that *Housekeeping* is not auto-biographical as far as characters, but your hometown of Sandpoint, Idaho, was used as a setting for Fingerbone. Could *Housekeeping* have been written using the sod-houses of Nebraska in the Great Plains where your grandfather grew up or is the Northwest setting crucial to the story?

MR: The importance of water is so great in *Housekeeping*. A lot of the book is a meditation on that lake and the memories that accompany it. I think without that lake it would necessarily have been a different book.

AV: Do you think where one grows up determines how one writes? For example, you grew up in the Northwest, your grandfather was from the Midwest, and you were edu-cated at Brown University in the Northeast.

MR: I have no idea. I think writers are so singular that it's very hard to say. You can't look at a landscape which has been written about as if you were seeing it for the first time. How we understand landscapes has an enormous amount to do with who has written about them, yet we think of it in the opposite order. We think Mississippi created Faulkner, although you could make as good of a case that for all purposes Faulkner created Mississippi.

I think the writers that really influenced me were the New Englanders. When I grew up in Idaho, I read *Moby Dick* and looked at Lake Pend Oreille or *Walden*. Even though the scale of the landscape is much bigger in one case and much smaller in the other, I appropriated what I wanted out of both of them and felt perfectly at ease doing it, having not seen either the Atlantic Ocean or Massachusetts. What I took from them had to do with my own particular setting in life and the accidental overlap of what they did and what I felt would be interesting to do.

AV: Early in the novel Ruth has a dream of walking on the lake, with the dead people reaching up for her in conjunction with her grandmother's obituary. Is this a foreshadowing of what is to happen at the end of the novel?

MR: I didn't know what was going to happen at the end of the novel until I wrote it. The book was very much composed as it occurs. The book ends in the way it does because of the subject it has. The subject pulls the book into its own shape and so at every point this is also true.

AV: Throughout the novel Ruthie and Lucille never seem to agree—whether it has to do with colors (e.g., the color of Sylvie's hair or the car their mother drove into Fingerbone Lake) or if their mother's death was intentional or not. Lucille is correct about the colors, whereas Ruthie is correct about their mother's death. Was this done intentionally to show that neither girl is always correct, thereby creating a certain ambivalence?

MR: I suppose what I had in mind more than anything else is that memory is unreliable. I don't want to sound tricky or anything, but it is Ruthie who's telling the story, which has something to do with what we take to be true.

AV: Right after Sylvie comes to stay with the sisters, Ruthie notices the similarity between Sylvie and her mother, so much so that "Sylvie began to blur the memory of my mother, and then to displace it." Shortly thereafter you write, "Memories are by their nature fragmented, isolated, and arbitrary as glimpses one has at night through lighted windows." These statements seem to recall Borges' comment in "Pierre Menard" that "error tries to tarnish memory." How do you conceive of time as it applies to both thought and relationships since it seems totally anomalous in *Housekeeping*?

MR: I don't know what memory is since memory appropriates things to itself and recreates itself constantly. I wouldn't say error tarnishes memory, but that memory is fluxile.

AV: In your essay "The First and Second Epistles General of Peter" you write, "The wrenching of time out of undifferentiated sequence is among the most brilliant accomplishments of the creators of biblical literature. For clearly there is a given-ness in things. Events do not occur in shapely forms as if they were the abstract of all possibility, or as if occasions were logical or Platonic structures that felt the pressure of chance and the tension of probability, and that energy flows toward event the way lightning pours through a fault in the atmosphere." In what ways is this statement, from both a biblical and literary context, applicable to your concept of time in *Housekeeping*?

MR: That's a tough question since I don't have the text of what I said about Peter in front of me. I think to the extent that I can be, I am influenced by contemporary thinking about time.

I have a great deal of respect for the new cosmology because there is no reason to have any particular loyalty for any earlier cosmology. The things we know about time apparently are true and descriptive and have to saturate our experience along with. everything else. It seems to me that's very interesting in terms of memory and experience because we have no reason to believe that outside ourselves in the cosmos there are point-by-point linearities, or any of these kinds of things. So, to the extent that we try to impose sequence and linearity on memory, we are falsifying them. It seems to me that the ways of thinking about time that are available to us scientifically, and obviously were available to very early writers in the Bible, that these are very pregnant ways of conceiving. They should be very much attended to and should not be considered secondary to or criticized by old notions of time and experience.

AV: Regarding the theme of time, there also seems to be a longing for some type of permanence, as shown when Ruthie and Lucille are making the snow lady statue: "Her shape became a posture. And while in any particular she seemed crude and lopsided, altogether her figure suggested a woman standing in a cold wind. It seemed we had conjured a presence." But despite her hope that "the lady would stand long enough to freeze," the statue falls apart. Is this statue supposed to symbolize Sylvie, who will become just another substitute mother figure, and what are your recollections about creating this scene?

MR: I don't really recall creating this scene in particular. It's hard to explain to people that writing fiction is a lot like painting. I came to that moment, and I thought what is implied here is, simply, a snow woman. It seemed to me necessary out of the prose. I think there are lots of things it connects with: it connects with the arrival of Sylvie; it connects with the image of Lot's wife; it connects with all kinds of other things. And, of course, the image of Lot's wife was suggested to me by the snow woman rather than the other way around. There is also the woman in the fallen house that she imagines, when she says she would have built a figure of snow, but those things are picking up on that image and doing it again. There is not a one-to-one relationship among these things. The snow woman exists fully in her own right. It just seemed to me a good thing to have in that place.

AV: Can you comment about the flooding of Fingerbone,

and the inherent symbolism, biblical and otherwise? For example, you state: "So Fingerbone, or such relics of it as showed above the mirroring waters, seemed fragments of the quotidian held up to our wondering attention, offered somehow as proof of their own significance."

MR: Floods are full of suggestion for me. The particular passage that you read had to do with an image that was in my mind of the flotsam that would be visible, thinking of the flood as a sort of silver tray with bits of flotsam on it. It seemed to me when reality was transformed in a radical way, that the value of everything was also transformed. Thus, rather than seeing things as ordinary, you see them suddenly in terms of the pathos of their temporality and impermanence. The cross itself would have been thought of as something crude or disgraceful or whatever. But by the transformation, by the re-evaluation, that came from the crucifixion, even a fragment of it, if it were an authentic fragment, would be transformed into something utterly different. That's the kind of transformation of the value, of worth, that was suggested to me.

AV: *Housekeeping* abounds with biblical allusions and metaphors—yet there are no blatant religious scenes where characters attend church or discuss the existence of God or one's mortality. Was this a conscious attempt not to have such scenes? And isn't *Housekeeping* essentially a parable illustrating a moral or religious theme in a contemporary setting?

MR: I would hesitate to call it a parable because I think parables tend to be misinterpreted. What parables *are* is misinterpreted. I don't think they seem the same way to me that they do to anybody else. If I were to refer to *Housekeeping* as a parable, I think that people would completely and systematically misunderstand what I meant by it. I don't think that people in general come anywhere near articulating in spoken language what they in fact think, not because they aren't honest, but because most of the deepest kinds of experience it never occurs to people to articulate. So the most essential issues of the novel are experienced at the level of consciousness and not in dialogue, just because that's the way the world seems.

AV: So was this a conscious attempt not to mention such scenes overtly?

MR: It never occurred to me to mention them. I hope the novel implies that something of the same scale and seriousness that goes on in Ruth's mind also goes on in the minds of all the people around her. That's the nature of the human landscape. I do think people have very profound lives of which they say virtually nothing.

AV: What about Sylvie's "housekeeping," the obsessive-compulsive nature and forgetfulness of her cleaning? This concept of housekeeping, from a psychological point of view, certainly depicts Sylvie as mentally unstable, but the sisters initially regard her behavior as merely eccentric. Why?

MR: I'm not crazy about psychological questions. This book is not about reality. I'm very uneasy making judgments about sanity and insanity in the real world, and I certainly wouldn't want to bring them into my book.

AV: The critic Paula Geyh in her article "Burning Down the House" states that "Sylvie mistakes accumulation for housekeeping—she understands the connection of housekeeping to the accrual of property, but not to the process of sorting and excluding, and so the parlor is filled with newspapers and cans stacked to the ceiling." Geyh later states the "floor and couch are littered with the dismembered remains of birds brought in by thirteen or fourteen cats, indicating a confusion of the boundaries between the outside and the inside, between natural and social space." *Housekeeping* in your novel entails both material and spiritual boundaries. Can you discuss your thoughts on these boundaries and the general role of the woman as housekeeper?

MR: I tried in *Housekeeping* to speak fairly respectfully of the whole phenomenon of housekeeping. The grand-mother, in particular, is a sort of artist in that form. I don't intend to create oppositions. In a way, Sylvie's housekeeping is a sort of variant of other people's house-keeping, in the sense that what is really accomplished in terms of accumulating things that matter and stabilizing environments and so on, is on a range between unsuc-cessful and even less successful. It's not as if anybody succeeds at this. It's just that Sylvie's failures are more obvious.

AV: There is a minor passage that discusses Sylvie's strange relationships with Edith (who dies in the boxcar) and Alma. What is the significance of this passage?

MR: Oh, I don't know. It's like the snow woman. I remem-ber thinking the passage was transforming a moment, which could be viewed in many other ways. I was thinking of Lincoln's funeral train, and of her spirit standing above her, which was her breath rising in the air. I wanted to establish dramatic and heroic suggestions which would transform the West, to put her life and death into another frame.

AV: Eventually, a split occurs between Lucille and Sylvie based on their respective approaches to life. This is high-lighted by Lucille's abhorrence of deterioration while Sylvie finds "fresh surprise" in the process and feels "the life of perished things." Doesn't this reflect Lucille's com-mitment to living in the everyday world whereas Sylvie acknowledges the impermanence of the physical world, with death providing the release from it?

MR: I think that throughout the book I've tried to criticize the distinction between the material world and the spir-itual world. It's not a distinction I habitually make my-self.

AV: There is the analogy of the sister's house and Sylvie's housekeeping to the lake where things are "massed and accumulated, as they do in combs or in the eaves and unswept corners of a house." Things become lost, misplaced, or forgotten, only to be discovered in a corner of the house or the flotsam of the lake. Does this indicate that, despite the fragmentary nature of things, there is some permanence or meaning to life?

MR: At that point the book is just pointing out analogies; how to interpret them is another question. On the one hand, at the physical level, insofar as the things matter to us, insofar as where they are constellated into objects and people, obviously there is no permanence. Or at least permanence as we perceive it. That's simply a datum. It doesn't mean there is a discontinuity between things to which we wish to attach permanence and the larger forces by which they are subsumed.

AV: Lucille dreams she is a baby and Sylvie is suffocating her with blankets, while Ruthie dreams she is waiting for her mother to return. Ruthie believes her dream is no less valid than Lucille's. Ruthie also believes we are deceived by appearances, so there is no difference between reality or dreams. Is this essentially true?

MR: I think, given the fact that all experience is internal, is mental experience, it's not possible to make secure distinctions about what's real and what's not real. Dreams obviously have an enormous potency and meaning and reality. I'm sort of tinkering with that. I think if there is one thing I'm doing in this book it's criticizing distinctions that seem more misleading than descriptive.

AV: The eventual split that occurs between Ruthie and Lucille is perhaps best expressed in the issue of education. Lucille eventually rejects Sylvie's tutelage and returns to high school and tells Mr. French her "attitude has changed," but Ruthie rejects the standard educational system in favor of Sylvie's teachings. Do you think

Ruthie is conscious of her decision to pursue a different type of education, or is it merely her closeness to Sylvie that draws her in that direction?

MR: I would hate to characterize her motives. Obviously she is very attracted to Sylvie. There are many other things which make Lucille's choices unattractive or unavailable to Ruthie, emotionally and otherwise. I would really hesitate to characterize her because the book is a fiction and Ruth's place in it is to express the active or kinetic space between the differences that Sylvie and Lucille represent.

AV: Perhaps the most important passage in the novel occurs when Ruthie and Sylvie take their boat trip to the remote valley. Can you comment on that strange conversation in the boat when Ruthie inquires about the children in the woods: "Have you ever seen any of them?" and Sylvie replies, "I think I have"?

MR: Nope.

AV: Ruthie feels the presence of the children as Sylvie did, but neither really sees any children when they are in the valley during their boat trip. Is the boat trip supposed to be a symbolic journey from earth to heaven, with the unseen children meant to represent the lost souls of the children? Or do the unseen children represent something else?

MR: It's not a journey from earth to heaven. I don't even submit to *that* distinction. It's very hard for me to say what those children represent. There is no direct equivalent for them in my mind. They are very highly charged for me with all kinds of things.

AV: There is that strange scene where Ruthie and Sylvie are sitting in the boat with the train going over them on the bridge, while underneath them at the bottom of the lake lies the train that Ruthie's grandfather died in. Is this supposed to represent a connection between the dead and the living?

MR: Certainly Sylvie is there because the train did go into the lake. The obsessions of the family are constellated around specific events, and that is a connection between the living and the dead.

AV: Ruthie also likens Sylvie to her mother, Helen, and calls out both their names to get a response from the person in the boat. Can you comment on this passage? Also, what is the inaudible statement Sylvie makes but when asked by Ruthie as to what she said she says, "Nothing"?

MR: I can't expound on the first question. Regarding the second question, the comment was inaudible so how can I know what she said?

AV: The Indian woman on the train responds to Sylvie's comment that Ruthie is a good girl by saying, "Like you always said." Who is this Indian woman supposed to be, since this is the only time she appears in the novel?

MR: Just herself. I think the most straightforward implication of the comment is certainly that Sylvie has not given up her transient ways.

AV: Ruthie states that she and Lucille were once "almost as a single consciousness," but later they grow apart. Then Sylvie says about Ruthie, "She's like another sister to me. She's her mother all over again." Then at the end of the novel, when the house is burning, Ruthie says about Sylvie and herself, "I think that night we were almost a single person." This shows Ruthie has completely separated from Lucille and now identifies with Sylvie (and, therefore, with her mother, Helen). Does this change in Ruthie indicate a spiritual transformation?

MR: I don't consider Ruth to be the only changing figure in an otherwise static situation. There's a lot of spiritual transformation.

AV: Sylvie is certainly not physically threatening to the community of Fingerbone; yet she is a threatening figure to them because she has a different concept of reality, as evidenced by her actions. Can you shed some light on why Fingerbone feels threatened and, conversely, why Sylvie doesn't feel threatened by their concept of reality?

MR: I think Sylvie feels somewhat threatened. But my intention, again, is never to establish hard distinctions. I think I've spent a fair amount of time drawing attention to the fact that Sylvie's sense of reality is very, very similar to the sense of reality of Fingerbone. She simply responds differently. The reason they feel alarmed about her is they understand perfectly well what she is thinking. She is *not* alien to them.

AV: There is such good characterization at work in *Housekeeping* since in the world of the book the reader tends to identify with Ruthie and Sylvie, while in the real world most of us would probably side with Lucille and the residents of Fingerbone as to what is normal. Do you agree?

MR: I don't think I would apply the category of "normal" to the people of Fingerbone as I represent them. I don't like loading situations, and I think people tend to villainize Fingerbone, which bothers me because I never intended it to be that way. The anxiety Fingerbone has about Ruthie is whether she is safe and minimally well, which are perfectly legitimate concerns for people to have, especially in the circumstances as things play themselves out. I don't think there is any suggestion in the novel, anywhere, that these people have some notion of conforming her to some elaborate, pre-existing idea of what is appropriate. They simply don't want her floating around on a glacial lake in the middle of the night in a leaking boat. It's not a monstrous anxiety that they are entertaining here.

AV: Toward the end of the novel the house is described as being "like a brain," at which point Sylvie and Ruthie try to burn the house (just as Sylvie burned the newspapers) in order to erase their memory. Thus, leaving the burning house seems to mean not only an end to housekeeping, but an end to their earthly existence. This seems to be confirmed by their running down the railroad tracks and disappearing into the night. Is this symbolically and metaphorically correct?

MR: It's not articulated in a way that makes one have to translate it. It's not as if it were symbolical or metaphorical. It means what it means. It is what it is. I don't acknowledge the need to translate out of a text into something that in effect would seem to be more clearly or more efficiently what the text says. Sometimes it has to be done out of necessity by critics or whatever, but I don't have to do it.

I don't want to imply that I'm simply leaving latitude for other people to make more authoritative interpretations than I'm willing to make. To my mind, and I thought about this considerably during the course of writing, the last scenes in the novel don't translate directly into any other kind of statement. That's what I wanted. In other words, I'm not trying to say something else in veiled language. I wrote those scenes for themselves. I don't want people to feel they have utter interpretative latitude, but I'm asking them to respond to these things as complex utterances and not try to eke them out into explanatory statements.

I think the person who said every art aspires to the condition of music was correct. I was trying to do what music does by having a great burden of implication without being reducible into a statement or program or idea.

AV: You could have concluded the novel as the movie version does, with Sylvie and Ruthie disappearing into the darkness as they run down the railroad tracks. So how did you derive that strange ending where Ruthie is still narrating the story as if she and Sylvie are still alive? And is this only in Lucille's memory?

MR: At the point where I was at that place in the novel it seemed right to me. It seemed to conclude what had come before it.

AV: The critic Allyson Booth states in a footnote to her

essay "To Caption Absent Bodies: Marilynne Robinson's *Housekeeping*" that "Ruth's text as a whole serves as a postscript to her own obituary." Doesn't this beg the question of how a deceased character can narrate her own story?

MR: That question again comes from the idea that fictions are impostures of a kind that attempt to produce something someone will mistake for reality. Fiction can do whatever it wants to do. There's no reason why I couldn't tell a story from the point of view of someone who wasn't born yet. People have done every kind of thing. It's a free country, the fictional country, very free indeed. You can do what you can get away with.

AV: What is your opinion of the criticism of your work? For example, critics such as Joan Kirkby and Paula Geyh cannot agree whether Ruth and Sylvie are still alive at the end of the novel. Does this give you a certain pleasure that critics come to different conclusions? Additionally, do critics sometimes point out certain motifs or elements of which you were previously unaware?

MR: Critics sometimes do point out things I never noticed before, and that's very funny. I heard a critical paper, by some strange accident, that pointed out neatly interlocking thematic things which I had never noticed. Maybe they are there. Maybe it was my subconscious doing all that bright stuff. And then there's the other side of that coin, which is that often things you really dislike are attributed to your work. Then the critics say you didn't do it consciously and it was your subconscious that was doing it. This is a kind of thing that makes one gnash one's teeth.

AV: Does that give you a certain pleasure that critics come to different conclusions?

MR: It's very rare that I read criticism of *Housekeeping*. I probably have read two or three articles that people have handed me. Of course anybody is flattered to be of interest to other people, but in terms of reading criticism, I don't read it.

AV: What did you think of the movie version of *House-keeping*?

MR: I liked the movie very much and thought Bill Forsythe did a great job directing. I thought Christine Lahti was excellent as Sylvie and that the actresses who played the girls [Sara Walker and Andrea Burchill] were very good.

I know that a lot of choices about the film were made in terms of how things would look on film, which is a very special problem. For example, Bill Forsythe's choice about where to end the film simply had to do with the difficulties of translating the ending I had written into visual equivalents. The book was not exactly what most people would think of as being a filmable book. Forsythe had to make a lot of choices that responded to that fact. I don't take exception to any of the choices he made. I think he did a marvelous job and made fairly recalcitrant material into a lovely film.

AV: What was your feeling about seeing your fiction trans-lated into another medium? Isn't it strange to see your memory and creative process not only put into words, but almost put into real life?

MR: It is strange. It's one of those experiences that little in life prepares you for, but on the other hand it always seemed to me to be Forsythe's film. Forsythe made a wonderful film, and I was very lucky. There are very few books that are made into films that come near being that satisfactory as film. It also seemed the movie was a sort of companion to my book rather than being something to be judged as a translation of my book. It didn't seem like my book being projected onto the screen; it seemed like something I was very familiar with but nevertheless was Forsythe's creation.

AV: There is the passage about Cain and Abel where you discuss the sense that someone's absence can become their presence. This can be construed on the physical level between the two sisters, but can't it also be viewed metaphorically and/or spiritually? For example, it could reflect the philosophy of Paul Tillich, who spoke of God's dynamic absence as also being a dynamic presence.

MR: I don't know if I have read that particular work of Tillich's, but I have been very interested in theology for a very long time, even before I wrote *Housekeeping*. I think that part of the reason American literature of the nineteenth century seized on my imagination is because it is saturated with theology. Those frames of reference are very much in my mind. I don't think it's fair to exclude any respectable and interesting theological idea that was available to me at that time.

AV: People change as they get older due to their experiences. Has your philosophical or theological thinking changed since you were in college or since you wrote *Housekeeping*?

MR: Yes, of course. It's my sense of reality that's changed. It's like when I was writing that piece about the epistles of St. Peter. I was struck by so many things in the epistles that I would never have been so sensitive to at an earlier age. I think my sense of reality, in regard to what the world is and what its prospects are, has been severely chastened. This is the area of greatest transformation.

AV: Essentially the Bible is used as a reference text for *Housekeeping*, and the interpretation of language is certainly important in both books. Do you think, however, that *Housekeeping* loses some of its value when interpreted by readers who are not religious or who do not believe in an afterlife?

MR: I have no way of knowing. There's no way of anticipating who will respond to what you write. I don't know what people's thinking is or where it comes from. I would never try to calculate or judge anybody's receptivity to anything I write.

AV: What part of the Bible influenced you the most in relation to *Housekeeping*? Do you see your writing as an extension of the Bible?

MR: It would be hard to say. I think it's obvious that I have always been very struck by the Old Testament. I have always been very struck by the New Testament. I wouldn't presume to extend it, but I would consider myself to be in the company of commentators.

AV: Do you subscribe to the premise of John Gardner's *On Moral Fiction*? Do you think fiction should have a moral point of view?

MR: I have never read that book. Everybody brings it up. I think I am in line with Old and New Testament traditions when I say that people who are too willing to assume that they know what morality is are probably in trouble. Openness and inquiry and graciousness of spirit are probably the things most to be cultivated.

I don't want to be dismissive of John Gardner any more than he wishes to be dismissive of other people. I do think things which are fundamentally generous in spirit are often taken to be immoral or amoral because they hesitate to disapprove. I really think everything has to be looked at in its own light.

AV: What do you think of Tom Wolfe's essay "Stalking the Billion-Footed Beast," which promotes writers of nonfiction and writers of the realist mode?

MR: I haven't read that either. People come up with these manifestos, and I'm sure they have some kind of value in the sense that they articulate positions. Realism is certainly the most artificial convention of all. It's fine, too, just like the rest of them are fine. Every book has to be judged on its merits. There is no reason to favor one kind of writing over another.

AV: There was a critic who made a comment about E.M. Forster when he was still alive that his reputation continued to grow with each book he didn't write. Do you see yourself in that light because you've written only one book of fiction? Why haven't you written more?

MR: I don't know. I guess I should be glad that E. M. Forster and I share this beatified state. I can't take my eyes off the world in a certain sense. I care about the writing of fiction, but not to the exclusion of learning. I spend a lot of time reading history. It's all important. I don't write unconsidered things. I do take my writing, and this is an understatement, seriously. I don't want to write as if just writing by itself were sufficient. Fiction is, however, the most important thing in my life. That's why I don't write all the time.

AV: In *Housekeeping*, there are no male characters of any real importance. In fact, if male characters had been used it most likely would have interfered with the storytelling and the relationships of the women. Were you aware of the lack of male characters when you wrote the book? Has there been any criticism and/or praise for a novel almost exclusively about women?

MR: People mention that *Housekeeping* is a story about women. I didn't intend to leave men out originally, but at a certain point I realized there were not going to be male characters, and I thought that's fine.

AV: *Mother Country* seems to have both a satiric and an ironic title, which condemns the British for allowing massive radioactive pollution from the Sellafield plant. How did you choose the title for your book?

MR: I don't know how those things come to mind. In both books, *Housekeeping* and *Mother Country,* there was just a certain point in writing the book where the title seemed to appear. I think that *Mother Country* comes from the fact that, when I was a child in first grade in Idaho, the first lesson in social studies was one sentence that said, "England is our mother country." I thought this was an odd piece of colonialism to be inflicted upon the children of Idaho.

AV: In the introduction to *Mother Country* you state you are "angry to the depths of my soul that the earth has been so injured." What brought this problem to your attention, and how did *Mother Country* evolve into a book?

MR: I was living in England in 1983, and I read about it in the newspapers and saw it on television. It was perfectly available to me at that time, basic facts and information. When I came back to the United States, I wrote an article which was published by *Harper's* and on the basis of that article I was asked to write a book. Most of the research I did was in libraries in New England—the point being that any reader who wanted to reproduce what I had done, to find out what my sources were and how reliable my interpretations of them were, could reconstruct it. It also makes the point that everything I wrote, although it's completely unknown at the level of general information, could be known without ever leaving a good library in the United States.

AV: You state in *Mother Country* that "a fiction writer has to braid events into a plausible sequence" whereas "news is simply a series of reported incidents." Was it difficult making the transition from fiction to nonfiction, and which genre is more satisfying?

MR: I had written a dissertation before, which was on Shakespeare. It made me very grateful for my academic background, which taught me how to do research and to write nonfiction.

Writing fiction and nonfiction are very, very different things. In both cases you have an enormous problem of trying to break out of received ideas. Aside from that, it's just a different problem. For example, with nonfiction you might be trying to show some kind of sophisticated loyalty to information, whereas with fiction you're trying to generate the thing out of whole cloth and those are very different kinds of problems.

AV: Do you find one genre more satisfying than the other?

MR: I like writing nonfiction, although I didn't like writing *Mother Country* because the subject matter wasn't pleasant. I'm happy writing nonfiction because I find things complementary. I have the illusion when I write nonfiction that things are less susceptible to misinterpretation.

AV: The Poor Laws in England, which were enforced for over five hundred years, had a Catch-22 effect by not letting people move to find work, even when no work was available locally. A similar Catch-22 is in effect with the Sellafield plant, which produces plutonium for profit while polluting the land and killing her people. This begs the question of whose interests are most important to the British government. Do you think the only way for Britain to prevent such problems is to abolish their system of socialism in favor of a more democratic system such as the United States has?

MR: The word "socialism" is problematic because Americans use it in two senses. They use socialism as it's presented in theory by people like Marx and Proudhon where the idea is there will be some kind of mutual commitment to collective well-being. Then you have actual historical regimes that call themselves socialist, like Russia and Britain. There's no evidence in history that they have attempted to promote collective well-being. What they have actually done is make a contemporary version of feudalism and call it socialism. Americans have made the odd mistake of interpreting Marx in terms of the practice of the Soviet Union or other regimes that were equally bizarre. But if you look at Marx himself, he's not describing anything that remotely resembles the Soviet Union or Britain or anything else. He wouldn't use the word socialism because he disliked British socialism so much. It was exactly what he did not intend as an example of his doctrine. Britain should be vastly more democratic than it is, but I don't think the opposition between socialism and democracy is appropriate. It's more like the difference between feudalism and democracy, what is going on there.

AV: *Mother Country* could be viewed as the nonfictional counterpart to Martin Amis' fiction in *Einstein's Monsters*. Strangely enough, an American attacks the British for nuclear pollution while a Briton attacks the Americans for promulgating the threat of nuclear holocaust. Do you see any irony in the fact that Americans and British are holding mirrors up for each other, but not looking at themselves?

MR: I don't think you can generalize from my book. I would be very interested to hear of another American book that criticizes British nuclear policy problems. There are many British books that criticize American nuclear policy. It's characteristic that Americans think anything bad that happens, happens in America, whereas the British think anything bad that happens, happens in America. And we seem to be predisposed to value their opinions. One reason that these very, very bad plants at Sellafield and elsewhere in Britain continue to operate is that Americans, for the most part, are not even aware of the fact they are there. Because we are so preoccupied with ourselves, Americans are not even aware that the British test their nuclear weapons in Nevada. Americans are typically not aware the British *have had* nuclear weapons for a very long time and *won't* subject them to arms control. We have acted as if only the United States and the Soviet Union are the only players in nuclear issues. This is a sad eccentricity of ours, this selective immunity to information.

AV: You said in an interview with Kay Bonetti that the audience for *Mother Country* was the United States, because our country was the best hope to exert a positive influence on Britain to stop their nuclear pollution. Since the book has been available for several years, has there been any response from America and has there been any attempt to close the Sellafield plant by the British?

MR: It's hard for me to know. I get a certain number of letters from people, and the fact that *Mother Country* sold fairly well shows that I've had some success in putting this information out. The British always are fussing about this plant. One day you hear they have a particularly high occurrence of cancer in the eyes of children around the Sellafield plant, but then an official comes out and says this is a coincidence. Then there is a particularly high incidence of bone cancer in children, and you have another excuse. There is always this sort of bubbling public relations problem that is associated with all the illness this plant causes. Then you might hear some murmurs of concern that maybe we shouldn't be doing this, but of course this goes on for twenty or thirty years and will go on forever as far as I can tell. The plant itself is expanding, and in the middle of the 1980s it was the largest construction project in Europe. Now of course a lot of the construction is done, which means all that gear they were putting in is now up and operating, so it's an expanding problem.

AV: I think you alluded in your book to the fact that there have been a lot of out-of-court settlements made with people who contracted cancer around Sellafield. It also seems that Ireland and other European countries would file law suits. Wouldn't all of these legal expenditures force the plant to shut down?

MR: The question always comes down to the amount of legal recourse people actually have. I described that part where out-of-court payments are made and this is set up so they will not have to go to court, supposedly. The government owns this plant, and they regulate the way in which it deals with its victims. There is no free-standing legal apparatus that can effectively oppose the government. As far as the Irish and many other European countries—they have had resolutions passed against the Sella-field plant but by the European Parliament—these things amount to nothing. They do nothing but ease public relations problems.

AV: It's ironic, because the British are not only polluting the Irish but part of their own country, not just in England, but in Northern Ireland.

MR: There's no question about it. The pollution is phenomenal because it has gone on for so long and on such a large scale.

AV: In your essay "Hearing Silence: Western Myth Reconsidered" you say, "A central myth of ours, if it were rendered as narrative, would sound like this: One is born and in passage through childhood suffers some grave harm. Subsequent good fortune is meaningless because of this injury, while subsequent misfortune is highly significant as the consequence of this injury. The work of one's life is to discover and name the harm one has suffered." First of all, to what degree of importance do you think great writing is a product of one's misfortune? Secondly, with all the harm that humanity has inflicted and endured, doesn't this imply great writing would be the product of malevolent times and that peaceful times would not spawn any writers of merit?

MR: The passage you quoted was intended very ironically. I would call it a mean little myth and say it is incompatible with art. The relationship of injury to art is that great art is fundamentally generous. The object of that generosity is often the overcoming of injury. The tendency of people to dwell on models of victimization, which makes them judge other people, simplistically and harshly, is something I abhor.

AV: In what way does your short story "Connie Bronson" reflect the statement, "One is born and in passage through childhood suffers some grave harm?" Is Connie Bronson based on a real person and incident in your life?

MR: As a matter of fact, she is based on somebody I knew in grade school when I was a little girl in Idaho. I visited her house once. How can you tell what will matter to you or how important these things will be later on in life? But there's a certain discomfort everybody feels with themselves, physically and so forth, and probably never more so than in childhood. "Connie Bronson" was written many years ago and actually predates *Housekeeping*, whereas "Hearing Silence" was written a year ago. I think "Connie Bronson" could be fairly described as a bit of juvenilia, if I could use that unkind language to talk about my own production.

AV: In "Hearing Silence" you also state, "Reading James Galvin's book, *The Meadow*, I was movingly reminded of the West of my memory. It occurred to me how intrinsic a part silence is of Western culture and experience, and how vulnerable they are to misinterpretation for that reason." Can you elaborate on this statement within the context of the essay as well as your fiction?

MR: It seems to me that if there is anything writing aspires to beyond the condition of music, it's probably the condition of silence. It's a hard thing to talk about. Silence as a positive aesthetic is something I'm very aware of. I think that silence might be a music rather than an absence of sound in the same way that space is a texture or filament of fabric and not an absence.

AV: In some ways, "Hearing Silence" is a continuation of *Mother Country*; that is, it deals with a country being blind to her own faults. For example, you state, "Americans are still so profoundly in awe of what they take to be their cultural origins that they cannot really criticize them." This implies a moral weakness and lack of courage in the collective consciousness of our country. What has caused this, and how can we correct such intangibles?

MR: I'm afraid we don't do better than we do because we

are human. I think we are very human in that even our best intuitions are not available to us all the time or at the right time. Every culture is riddled with oddness and error, and we are, too. What I particularly wanted to do in that book was to make Americans less immune to information and able to read a newspaper in a foreign country. I have no evidence that I accomplished my goals. My hopes were basically modest. I don't think the United States will be able to solve the human tragedy for ourselves or for anybody else.

Examining the Disease

Hubert Selby, Jr.

HUBERT SELBY, Jr., the son of an engineer, was born on July 23, 1928, in Brooklyn, New York. He attended Peter Stuyvesant High School for one year before shipping out with the merchant marines from 1944 to 1946. During the late 1940s, he contracted tuberculosis and was in the hospital for three and a half years. Later he was jailed for drug use. He held various jobs, which included working as an insurance analyst and a freelance copy writer for the *National Enquirer*. His first book, *Last Exit to Brooklyn*, was banned in England and Italy.

Works published to date include *Last Exit to Brooklyn* (1964), a collection of six semirelated stories; *The Room* (1971), a novel; *The Demon* (1976), a novel; *Requiem for a Dream* (1978), a novel; and *Song of the Silent Snow* (1986), a collection of short stories.

The first time I encountered Selby, I was in graduate school doing research on another writer. While perusing some microfiche, I ran across a story in the *Provincetown Review* titled "Tralala." I recall the initial shock of reading his extremely graphic prose and the feeling that each word of his stream-of-consciousness style was catapulting the reader to read even faster. When I finished reading "Tralala" and the horrific ending that befalls the protagonist, my heart was racing.

Immediately thereafter I purchased *Last Exit to Brook-*

lyn and *The Room*. Reading these books confirmed that
Selby has his own inimitable style. In fact, critics sometimes
find it frustrating because there does not seem to be a group
of writers with whom he can be lumped.

Fifteen years had elapsed when I noticed in the newspaper that *Last Exit to Brooklyn* was being made into a
movie (starring Jennifer Jason Leigh in an engaging performance as Tralala) that was to be released first in Europe
before making it to America. Reading this newspaper clip-
ping spurred my interest in Selby again, whereupon I contacted his agent and tracked him down in West Hollywood.

The interview with Hubert Selby was conducted on November 18, 1989. Mr. Selby spoke by phone from his home
in West Hollywood. He was very adamant about getting his
point across and expressed disappointment that his fiction
did not receive the credit that it should have. He was working on a project titled *Seeds of Pain, Seeds of Love* at the
time, but since then he has gone back to work on a manuscript he started thirteen years ago called "The Willow
Tree."

AV: You were born, raised, and educated in Brooklyn.
    What effect did that environment have on your writing?
HS: There is really no way of knowing for sure if any
    writer's environment has an effect on your writing. There
    is no way of determining that, because you can't do a
    controlled experiment. I think one of the biggest influ-
    ences of being born and raised in a city like New York is
    that it gave me a universal appreciation. A lot of people
    in Europe consider me European. I didn't understand
    why until I moved to Los Angeles. I can see why Los
    Angeles is really an American city, whereas New York is
    very international. I think growing up in New York is the
    best gift you can have living in this country.
       My mind was opened to a lot of things I wouldn't have
    otherwise known. I believe the biggest influence of grow-
    ing up in New York was that it made me very responsive

to speech and the music that there is in speech. I write by ear, and the music of speech fascinates me. I don't think you have that in the rest of the country. You don't have the incredible diversity of music you have in the speech of New York. It doesn't make any difference if someone's ethnic background is Greek, Italian, or Jewish, whereas if they live outside New York they would all sound flat, like the Midwest. In New York, you couldn't begin to describe the different flavors of speech. Consequently, I think the music of New York speech has been a big influence on my writing.

AV: How did you develop your writing style, which sometimes resembles a stream-of-consciousness paper from a creative writing class?

HS: That I wouldn't know, never having gone to school, praise God. It's hard to say exactly. We are never really aware of as much as we believe we are aware of, because self-deception is part of the human condition. I think my writing style, as I've said, is a product of my fascination with speech and the music of speech. I am not too concerned with the physical environment but with what goes on *inside* a person. This is really important to me, because I realize it is what goes on in our heads that creates the world we live in. So the stream-of-consciousness just comes naturally, I believe. I have, of course, read Joyce and have been influenced by him. I think every writer who has read Joyce has been influenced one way or another by his work. But it's the interior dialogue that we have with ourselves that really fascinates me and how it is reflected in our physical world. Maybe that is why my writing at times looks like it is a stream-of-consciousness.

AV: I understand you contracted tuberculosis and spent three years in the hospital, had ten ribs cut out, lung problems, and asthma. How has illness and a sense of your own mortality affected your writing and your outlook on life?

HS: You spend three and a half years in bed, and it affects

your life, and everything that affects your life affects your work. I also believe that you don't understand life until you die or come close to dying. That may have a lot to do with the nature of my writing. Lying in bed also gives you a greater opportunity than usual to look inside yourself and find out exactly what's going on. I had never read a book until then. That's where it all started: reading, and then a desire to write.

AV: Did you find it difficult to get your stories published in the beginning? Is it still hard to get published?

HS: I never really tried to get published. I knew people who suggested I send it here or there. I followed their advice and got published in the *Black Mountain Review* and *Provincetown Review*. The same thing happened with the books. I don't know whether I have more trouble getting published today or not. In this country, not too many people want to have anything to do with me. That could be translated into having a problem getting published.

AV: Why do you suppose a lot of people don't want to have anything to do with you? Because of the fiction? Because it's not commercial?

HS: I have to assume they are frightened by something. For example, I recently read an article in the *Smithsonian*. It was about writers who are associated with Brooklyn, and they listed writers like Tom Wolfe and Henry Miller, but I was not on the list. You can hate a writer, but how can you not include my name with a list of writers associated with Brooklyn? That's the attitude of the literary establishment toward me in this country.

AV: What writers influenced you?

HS: There are a lot of writers I admire, but as to who influenced me, it's hard to say. One of the reasons it's difficult is that when I started reading, I read everybody at once, which was a great advantage because I didn't have to work under the influence of any writer. For example, I didn't have to write like Hemingway, but later on Steinbeck, Faulkner, and Hemingway certainly influenced me and, to a lesser degree, Mickey Spillane. There also seems to me a very close kinship to Celine in my work. I remember reading *Thais* by Anatole France. It just knocked me over, and I'm sure that had a tremendous influence on me. William Saroyan, I remember, also knocked me out.

Obviously, James Joyce—and especially William Carlos Williams. I have no way of knowing how much Williams influenced me, but he did, not the least of which is his use of the American language and his insistence on its rhythms. Isaac Babel was a tremendous influence. I also like Gilbert Sorrentino, Richie Price, Michael Stevens, and Joseph Ferrandino, who wrote a book about Vietnam called *Firefight*. I adore the work of Joseph Heller. Unfortunately, I don't get to read as much as I'd like, so I'm not too familiar with all the writing that is going on.

AV: Are the recurring character names in *Last Exit* and your subsequent fiction based on real people? If so, did they know they were being written about? Any knowledge of their whereabouts thirty years later?

HS: The people were real in the sense that they're not totally fictionalized people. I create real people in my books, but there was no Harry Black or Tralala. Actually, there was someone named Tralala, but I never saw her or met her. I just overheard a conversation between two guys in the Greek's saying, "Remember that time Tralala put her tits on the bar?" Later on someone said something about finding Tralala naked in the lot. I don't even know if Tralala was her real name or a nickname.

AV: What about Tony and Vinnie?

HS: They're based on hundreds of Tonys and Vinnies I've known in my life, but the interesting thing you were asking about thirty years later is that there were three guys from that neighborhood around the army base that came down to the movie set. We had a reunion where we discussed the old days in the '50s and '60s. Each of them had read all or part of the book, and they all had the same reaction: "This never happened!" or "This ain't the way it was!" In a sense, it's all based on reality and on my experience as it goes through my imagination, but there is no Harry Black or Tralala or any specific person it was based on.

AV: Many of your characters are intrinsically angry—angry at everybody in particular and society in general. Do they embody your own sense of personal rage?

HS: Yes. During that time, anger was the only thing I was aware of, but I had no idea how much I loved these people I was creating. I became really aware of it watching the film *Last Exit to Brooklyn* being made and looking at the finished product. I do remember it took me six years to write *Last Exit*, and it was a real struggle. I remember when I would finally finish a piece and the people would end up in the terrible places they end up, then I would quite often pass out. I think by the time I had finished "Tralala," I spent two weeks in bed. I really got involved with my characters, and I lived and died with them. I was enraged at everything and, to the best of my ability, I directed all my rage and anger toward God, because that was the son of a bitch who did this to me.

AV: Is it your aim for the readers to incorporate the anger in your fiction, albeit unconsciously, into the real world of their own lives?

HS: I don't know if what you mean by "incorporate into the real world" means to go out and be angry with someone you weren't angry with before. I've never heard of that happening. The people who talked to me about *Last Exit* all use the same word regarding their reaction to the book, and that's "compassion." This was not a conscious intention of mine as I wrote *Last Exit*, but one of the results of the book, from what everyone tells me, is they feel compassion for these people and they end up loving people whom they previously felt were unlovable. It's a great thing to happen, and I think the same thing happened with the film.

AV: Do you see your writing as an extension of the Angry Young Men writers, such as Sillitoe and Osborne, in England in the '50s?

KS: I don't believe so. I haven't read them extensively. They were socially conscious people making a social statement. I am not.

AV: In *City of Words: American Fiction 1950–70*, Tony Tanner says: "A good way to describe what Selby is doing is to say that he is trying to depict a human version of what the ecologist John Calhoun called a 'behavioral sink.' In a 'behavior sink' all normal patterns of behavior are disrupted, and the unusual stress leads to all forms of perversion, violence, and breakdown." Is this an accurate assessment?

HS: I don't think in those terms. I'm not trying to depict a human version of anything. I am doing the best I can to create real people. Now maybe these people fall into this category as this man perceives it. My intent, however, is to put the reader through an *emotional experience* and not have him just read stories. I have to write from the inside out. Now, if in doing that, it ends up these people fall into what this guy categorizes as a "behavioral sink," then maybe it is true, but it was never my intent.

AV: One of the major problems your characters experience is a lack of communication, and whatever communication there is seems to occur in a sea of obscenities and anger. Why do your characters persist in such impossible relationships?

HS: I think that's what this guy is referring to when he says a "behavior sink." My characters live in a fictional hell because that is the way the world is. You defend by attacking. We do that as individuals and as couples be-

cause we don't communicate with ourselves. If we are
not communicating properly with ourselves, how are we
going to do it with another human being? If we can't do it
as individuals and couples, how can we possibly do it as a
nation? It's easy to look at what the politicians have done
in the last twenty years and see how communication is so
faulty that it's destroying the world. It's very easy to see
this, but not quite so easy to see it within ourselves and
how I miscommunicate with myself. That's the thing that
fascinates me. We believe what is true is false and what is
false is true. I don't really go out to hurt you or hurt me,
but I believe I'm doing something that's going to make
me feel better.

AV: Some of your characters—who evoke some of the most
sadistic, cruel, and lowest standards of human behavior—get their comeuppance at the end (e.g., Tralala in
her story and Harry Black in "Strike"). Do you believe
your characters, as well as people in real life, deserve to
be punished?

HS: I don't believe in punishment. Punishment is a religious
concept that has nothing to do with the reality of my
being. When I'm communicating with myself, I know I
am not guilty. I know sin does not exist. Therefore, there
is no need for punishment. I absolutely do not believe in
punishment. I guess it's called karma. I don't know anything about it, but I do know there is a cause for every
effect. It seems our world, especially religious people,
really believes in punishment. (I've been a member of
Amnesty International and of the Urgent Action Net-
work, for whom I've been writing to heads of state for a
long time.) The response of people is that they really
believe in punishment. They do not believe in the correction of errors because they believe in sin. So they must
punish people. Look at Jerry Falwell or the Ayatollah
Khomeini and see what they believe in, see what they
propose. They want punishment. No, I don't believe in

punishment. I believe in the correction of mistakes. It's my mistakes that I can correct. It's my duty and obligation to be willing to do that.

AV: How did you choose the title *Last Exit to Brooklyn*?

HS: The title comes from a sign on the Belt Parkway as it goes from Brooklyn into Queens. There is an exit sign which says "Last Exit to Brooklyn." There is also another sign at the other end just before you go into the Brooklyn Battery Tunnel that says "Last Exit to Brooklyn Street."

AV: "The Queen is Dead" is a pathetic story of a hip queer looking for love, but all Georgette finds is sarcasm, hate, and violence. Typically, the reader would be sympathetic to the narrator, but do you think most readers are when Georgette is a weak-willed, speed-freak transvestite?

HS: It depends upon how well the reader communicates with themselves. If they insist upon denying that there is a bit of Georgette in them, then I guess they would have to attack Georgette just as Vinnie and Harry do. They weren't willing to accept that Georgette exists within you and me. Perhaps my attitude is a little different, but I can see the terrible hunger for acceptance in motivating and perverting Georgette's behavior.

AV: What was the basis for writing "The Queen Is Dead," and how were you able to write from the mental perspective of a drag queen?

HS: I don't see how it's so difficult. Look at how many male writers have written great female literary characters. That's something very personal with Georgie and myself. I didn't know it at the time, but I identified with Georgie from the inside. I realize now that Georgie felt like an outcast.

AV: So Georgette was based on an actual person?

HS: There was a real kid named Georgie. Georgie must have felt like an outcast who was totally alienated. He was hysterical in his defense—and his defense was his hysteria. And the more he fed that with stimulants, the more hysterical and wacky and flighty he became. I've always felt like an outcast who was alienated all my life. So Georgie and I had that point of identification, although this was totally unconscious. I had a tremendous sympathy for Georgie. I felt like my life was fucking ruined and a disaster. So I had this empathy, sympathy, and compassion going for Georgie.

I wrote the first part of that story, which is one of the first things I ever wrote, from the beginning up until Georgie gets stabbed and they take him home. Originally, the story was called "Love's Labours Lost." A year or two later I met someone from the old neighborhood, and they said Georgie had been found dead in the street, evidently an O.D. He was only about twenty years old when he died. I was very, very moved by that information—so much so that I finished the story. I guess I felt Georgie needed more than to be just a death in the street. He needed a memorial. So I finished the story, which in turn led to my writing the entire book. Thus, in a very real way, Georgie is responsible for the book *Last Exit to Brooklyn*.

AV: Portions of *Last Exit To Brooklyn* were copyrighted as early as 1957—yet drugs are mentioned frequently in your writing. What was your exposure to drugs (long before it became fashionable in the '60s), and do you write under the influence of drugs or alcohol?

HS: I never write under the influence of anything. I tried it briefly. The last part of the "Queen Is Dead," where Georgette is dying of an O.D., I tried sipping beer a couple of times and I tried a little Demerol, but I just couldn't do it and that is the only time I tried to write under the influence.

When I was in the hospital, I had a lot of drugs such as morphine, Demerol, codeine, and various sleeping pills. I also used heroin. I also drank every opportunity I could, so I had that point of reference, but I never wrote under the influence.

AV: The story "And Baby Makes Three" centers on an un-caring society of parents—to wit, Suzy, who, two weeks after having a baby, doesn't give it a second thought while she parties until it's time to leave: "So she hunted around and found the kid and cutout." Why do most of your characters who have kids treat them so badly?

HS: I don't know the exact root of that, except I've felt victimized and alienated all my life. I've come to terms with that, and I realize feelings aren't necessarily facts. I was always very sensitive. There seemed to be a lot of that stuff when I was a kid—kids being battered and banged around. I don't know why I've always been so fascinated by that. I used to give things away to kids because I thought they didn't have anything. I have no idea why.

It has always pissed me off why parents have kids and then treat them so badly. I mean, for Christ's sake, the kid's response should be, "I didn't ask to be born. What the fuck are you on my back for?" I'm sure every kid has had the same experiences I've had. You can't reach a doorknob by yourself. You can't get a glass of water. You are totally dependent on the adult world. Yet, the attitude of the adult world is, "Get out of the way, kid, you bug me."

AV: The first three sentences of "Tralala" say a lot about the title character: "Tralala was 15 the first time she was laid. There was no real passion. Just diversion." Most readers would expect a girl's first sexual encounter to be special, but Tralala, in the world of Selby, is incapable of feeling. How did you create Tralala?

HS: I suspect we all feel the same way. One way or another, most of us are trying to defend against our feelings. We don't want to feel them, we don't want to interpret them, and we don't want to feel guilty. We want to try and project that guilt on someone else. I think we start at an early age to protect ourselves from our feelings.

I believe a story is given to me, and it is up to me to

understand the essence of that story. It's a responsibility. It took me two and a half years to write "Tralala," which is only about twenty pages long. Most of that time was spent trying to understand the story. When I finally did understand what my responsibility was, then the story just flowed. This is what I was supposed to do with the story: to reflect the psychodynamics of an individual to the rhythm, beat, and tension of a prose line. I understood this to be my task. You previously mentioned that "Tralala" starts with a very tight, short kind of beat and then the line gradually opens up more and more until she reaches the apex of her life where the line is almost a normal line and then the line starts to fall apart. You expect it to disappear any second, but it keeps going on until the end. It never ends. It just stops.

AV: Tralala also is capable of great cruelty. For example, after Tony and Al have beaten up a seaman, Tralala, for no reason at all, "stomped on his face until both eyes were bleeding his nose was split and broken then kicked him a few times in the balls." Why?

HS: I'll tell you what Buddha would say. "Don't ask why. Why is not important."

AV: Tralala gets her comeuppance in the end after she has been gangbanged countless times: ". . . so they continued to fuck her as she lay unconscious on the seat in the lot . . . (the kids) tore her clothes to small scraps put out a few cigarettes on her nipples pissed on her jerked off on her jammed a broomstick up her snatch . . . Tralala lying naked covered with blood urine and semen and a small blot forming on the seat between her legs as blood seeped from her crotch." Please comment on what may be the most vividly disgusting passage in the annals of literature.

HS: I guess the Christians would say Tralala collected the wages of sin. The Hindus would talk about karmic law. Maybe it's more important for us to see the results to understand some of the spiritual principles underlined.

Tralala does get her comeuppance in the end, even though she was raped. A rape doesn't occur if you're insisting on it, but she didn't know what she was insisting on—again, this miscommunication with one's self. She didn't start out to get herself gangbanged, but she made a conscious decision to inflict pain on Annie and Ruthie. She resented them and tried to ruin their good thing with Jack and Fred. Tralala was projecting that anger on them, but her anger finally caught up with her. That's the law of the universe.

AV: The story "Strike" shows Harry Black as another pathetic character incapable of goodness, who only feels good when other people are miserable. Harry isn't happy until he makes love to the transvestite Alberta. Why are love and happiness often equated in perverted scenes for most of your characters? Is there anything normal in Selby's world of fiction?

HS: First of all, to get the record straight, we can't pervert our concept of love. For instance, we have these great church leaders in this country and other countries, such as Iran, who say people should be murdered. That's not love to me, and yet they claim to be teaching love in the name of God. Now, the perversion of it is something we live with and deal with all the time. I believe *Last Exit* is a microcosm of our world from the beginning of time and will continue till the end of time. I see that perversion of love everywhere. I think it's really dramatized in the book and magnified many times. I also see that perversion permeating in what the U.S. has done politically in Nicaragua, El Salvador, Vietnam, and elsewhere.

AV: Harry Black, who is seemingly incapable of crying, starts to cry when he is brutally beaten after he tries to have sex with ten-year-old Joey. Harry's last words are, "God You Suck Cock." It seems incongruous that Harry is now capable of feeling but blames God for the condition of the world.

HS: Anger is an attempt to make somebody else feel guilty.

Ultimately, Harry's last act is to accuse God of this problem. It is very simple and very logical.

AV: It seems you have a low opinion of religion.

HS: I don't believe in organized religion. I don't believe it is possible to seek spiritual principles and to make spiritual progress within an orthodox, organized religion. I'm certainly not in accord with what organized religion has done since the beginning of religion. Certainly more people have been murdered in the name of God than under any other guise.

I no longer resent them or blame them. I understand that I must love them as much as I love my children; otherwise, I am doing what I accuse them of doing. That's one of the laws of the universe. I try not to use the word "God" because there is such a misconception around that word. I do believe in a power that created and maintains the universe. I believe in a power of infinite and unconditional love, simply because that power has revealed itself to me from within me. Now I attempt on a daily basis to commune with this power and to live according to the spiritual principles that it dictates. That is my life.

AV: *Last Exit to Brooklyn* has finally been made into a movie twenty-five years after the novel was published. What are your thoughts about the movie?

HS: It was received very well in Europe where it opened on the twelfth of October 1989 in Munich. It is scheduled to open in the U.S. around March or April of 1990. I think the film is really great because it does justice to my fictional work. This may be one of the few times it has been done. We did not change the dark, oppressive nature of the book and thus remained faithful to the basic spirit of the book. The film consisted of an American cast and crew and was shot on location in Brooklyn, but the producer and director are German. Tralala was played by Jennifer Jason Leigh, Harry Black is played by Stephen

Lang, Vinnie is played by Peter Dobson, and Joe is played by Burt Young. It's a real ensemble where no one character or personality prevails. I played the driver of the car that kills Georgette.

AV: What was your basis for *The Room*? Didn't you spend some time in jail?

HS: I did spend a couple months in jail, but the basis for *The Room* is variations on a musical theme. You have a theme of the prisoner's reality, which includes such variations as his memory of it and his projections. You might call it an enigma variation. I wrote a story in jail called "The Sound," and that is where the concept for the novel started. It was published in my most recent book, which is a collection of stories entitled *Song of the Silent Snow*.

The reason I was in jail was for possession of narcotics. Heroin. The actual charge was driving while under the influence. The drugs were an extension of all the addictive medication I had when I was in the hospital. I haven't had any drugs now for more than twenty years.

AV: The unnamed prisoner in *The Room* is the antithesis of the prisoner in Camus' novel *The Stranger*. Whereas Camus' Meursault is ambivalent and fatalistic, your prisoner is filled with anger but has no way to release it. How were you able to sustain this anger and transfer it to the page?

HS: I know enough about anger to be able to remember the experience of it. You pay a price for it, I can tell you.

I tried to write from the inside out. I wanted to put the reader through an emotional experience, which means I must experience every emotion I'm writing in order to get it down to the point that the reader will experience it. I've spent a lot of time inside my head, and I understand the rage and frustration of being confined, not just in jail, but also the three and a half years in the hospital due to tuberculosis.

AV: *The Room* is written in such a manner that it is sometimes difficult to distinguish reality from the prisoner's fantasy.

HS: Initially, the reader may have a problem, but I believe once you get in the rhythm of the writing it becomes pretty obvious. I think the rhythm reveals everything so the reader can easily distinguish reality from fantasy.

AV: What was the reason for indenting the paragraphs more so than normal?

HS: Some of them are dropped paragraphs, but all my typography is musical notation. If it's indented more than usual and not a dropped paragraph, it's because I want that extra dotted note there.

AV: What was the stimulus for the brutal rape of Mrs. Haagstromm? Also, the original rape scene is part of the prisoner's fantasy, but later it appears to be part of the court testimony.

HS: The rape of Mrs. Haagstromm is a product of the prisoner's fantasy, where he attempts to destroy the prosecution and the cops. The rape scene is a product of his imagination to prove the authorities are really guilty and not him.

AV: How did you select Mrs. Haagstromm's name?

HS: I don't know. If you notice, the other names are like Hollywood soap opera names, whereas Haagstromm seemed to be a perfect name for a perfect person. It seemed totally appropriate.

AV: Mrs. Haagstromm, an innocent rape victim, seems to dramatically contrast with Tralala. However, you stated in an interview in the *Review of Contemporary Fiction*, "We all cause everything that happens to us, whether we recognize it or not." Does this apply to Mrs. Haagstromm?

HS: Everything that happens to us happens as a result of a decision we make, but she didn't necessarily make that decision, because she was a figment of the prisoner's imagination.

AV: It seems the prisoner becomes just as vindictive and sadistic as the two cops when he fantasizes about getting even with them. Essentially, the prisoner and the cops have the same mentality, don't they?

HS: Yes. Experiments have proven, since the book was written, that this is true.

AV: Discuss the scene where the prisoner fantasizes about having sex in church with Mary and the interplay of sex with the "Our Father."

HS: It just flowed perfectly and naturally from his psyche. It seems to be the most, as I'm thinking about it now, simple way again of accusing God of his problems. This guy is saying essentially the same thing as Harry Black: "Fuck God!"

AV: *The Room* also recalls the writing of Jean Genet's *Our Lady of the Flowers*, where the main character is in jail and draws an outline of his penis on a letter to his girlfriend. Please comment on Genet and such scenes in *The Room*: "It was as if that's all there was to him. As if that was all there was to be seen. Just a limp, sticky, scraping penis floundering around between his legs. And he had to walk behind it, slowly moving one leg and then the other, and follow it wherever it led him. It wasn't a part of him. He was a part of it."

HS: That was where he couldn't think above his navel, but I don't think Genet influenced that in any way. That's an awareness that you come to when you spend a lot of time locked up. I spent four years of my life locked up, both in the hospital and jail, and you become aware of where your mind goes.

AV: *The Room* ends with the prisoner basically imprisoned in his own mind. The novel seems to have come full circle to the beginning where the prisoner talked about astronomers and time: "And where did it get them? So they figured out where mars would be in ten thousand years. Big deal! Krist, what a stupid waste of time. And where did it get them? Where? After they figure all that shit out theyre either dead or still sitting on their ass looking at the goddamn sky. Right back where they started from. You always end up where you started from."

HS: Whether you look at it realistically or metaphysically, you end up from where you started. You have to get back to the beginning where you created the mistakes.

AV: Is the prisoner insane at the end?

HS: I don't think so. Not insane in the worldly sense, but we all are insane because we have all taught ourselves that what is true is false and what is false is true. I believe that's a form of insanity, perhaps not in this world, but metaphysically. What the prisoner is saying at the end of the book is that he is really a prisoner of guilt. Specifically, most of his guilt is sexual guilt because everything in his head is due to sexual repression. He is interpreting all of life sexually and using it viscerally and vindictively. There is no love in that book, but there is a lot of sex and violence. Sex is used as a power tool, but never as an expression of love. The guy is obviously feeling guilt. Whether or not he actually did something is immaterial, because he has found himself guilty. At the end of the novel they open his cell door and tell him to come out, but he says no since he has judged himself, like mankind, to be guilty even though we are born innocent.

AV: With the novel *The Demon* you have a character, Harry White, who is initially the opposite of the character Harry Black in "Strike." Yet, he chooses evil. Why do your characters, most of whom fail from a lack of mental control over their physical impulses, consistently choose evil when the alternative is the more obvious path to a satisfying life?

HS: For one thing, they don't *choose* evil. I don't think anyone deliberately chooses evil. If you will notice, the epitaph of that book says, "A man obsessed is a man possessed by a demon." We are dealing with obsessions of the mind, and the one basic quality about an obsession is that an obsession can never be satisfied. If your obsession is whiskey, there isn't enough whiskey in the world to satisfy you. There isn't enough money or power or women to satisfy you. An obsession can never be satisfied. What Harry attempts to do is to get free of the basic obsession by becoming obsessed with other things. At one point, I think he uses plants, and, for a while, he directs all his energies to becoming a successful businessman. All these things work, but only for a while. As far as he is capable, he loves his wife and his family, but since he must satisfy his obsession, then he has to surrender to it.

AV: It is unfortunate that John Gardner died so young because it would be interesting to have the two of you discuss his book *On Moral Fiction*. Do you think both of you are attacking the same problem from different poles? Also, what do you think of Gardner's book?

HS: That is something I'd love to discuss. The object, goal, and concern when I write is the perfection of my art. I try to write the best story I can write—how my personality is always involved with my sense of morality. I think you can see where one of my basic obsessions in life is love, the perversion of love, and the lack of love. You can also interpret what Gardner says as meaning we should be moral propagandists. I certainly don't believe that. I don't want to try and prove a point. If there is any point to be proven, the people that I create will prove and make that point. I believe the primary concern and responsibility of the artist is to be free of the human ego. So I don't think I have any business being in the book.

AV: There is a statement from John O'Brien's interview in the *Review of Contemporary Fiction* that says he believes Selby "can write so much about sex without being erotic." I think, however, many readers find your scenes with Tralala or the rape of Mrs. Haagstromm very erotic, if not perverse.

HS: I don't think of my writing as being erotic. I guess if you associate sex with violence and look at it as a power play or manipulation, then I guess maybe it is erotic for some people.

AV: Sex in your fiction is often an act of desperation. Do you think this is basically true of sex in general?

HS: Yes. I think sex, when performed as an act of desperation, is a very basic instinct and it is an instinct for survival. Ironically, sex as an act of desperation often leads to reproduction and more desperation.

There is a lovely scene in a story by Faulkner called "Pylon," which is set in the old barnstorming days of pilots flying back in the '30s. It's about a guy who is supposed to do a parachute jump with his girlfriend. She is climbing out on the wing, but she has never done it before and she becomes frightened. She starts to crawl back into the cockpit where the guy is flying, and she grabs his fly and tries to rip his fly open. I think that is an instinctual thing with us when our lives are threatened. We reach for our crotch.

AV: Regarding sex as an act of desperation, the one possible exception I see in your work is the story "Landsend" where Abraham is almost fucked to death by Lucy. It concludes with Abraham and Lucy grinding away, both of them very content.

HS: Even though Abraham and Lucy have a good time fucking all night doesn't mean there isn't desperation. Look at Abraham's whole day and what is the focus of his entire being. It is all sex and thinking about this fine, brown-skinned girl. It seems to me there is a great deal of desperation there. For example, when he comes home he is exhausted, but after he hangs up his clothes and puts on his hairnet it's not because he's going to work the next day. And how about his wife? She's certainly bitching about her desperation because she's reaching for his crotch after fantasizing earlier about finding another cock. Desperation manifests itself in their lives through sex.

AV: *Requiem for a Dream* shows the addiction of four characters, with three of them hooked on heroin. While the novel can be approached as a microcosm of society, in hindsight, it seems virtually prophetic, with so many people addicted to crack cocaine and the overwhelming impact on society in terms of addiction, crime, and violence.

HS: We are all dealing with mental obsessions and, in this case, the "Great American Dream": if you make it on the outside then everything is going to be fine. It's not true. I don't care how limited or how infinite your dream may be. Success is an inside job because life is an inside job. (Perhaps I'm too involved with America, but it seems like we are more involved with facade than any other country because the influences of Madison Avenue and Hollywood are so persuasive and so powerful.) I think it becomes pretty obvious, whether it's Sara or Marion, regardless of what values we may have adopted. We still have this obsession to look for anything that will quiet the raging in our heads.

AV: "A Penny for Your Thoughts" (from *Song of the Silent Snow)* shows Harry fantasizing about the girl Marie. This story is representative of a lot of your fiction in that your characters prefer to fantasize about doing something rather than actually doing it.

HS: It seems to me there are a couple of things involved. First of all, in fantasy *I'm the boss*. Nothing else really impinges itself or can interfere with my fantasy. Whatever I want to do, I can do. Fantasy is safe. I don't have to take any chance of failure. However, if I try to bring this to life in the outside world, then I'm taking the chance of failure. We are also dealing with a very basic spiritual, metaphysical, psychological type of love. Remember, it was Jesus who said: if you go to bed with a married woman, you are committing adultery, and, *even if you think it*, you've committed it. Now that's a very interesting thing. I don't believe he was just making some kind of judgment, but was explaining the nature of life with that remark. Because we do create the world we live in with our thoughts. When I am continually fantasizing about doing something my inner self says, "Hey, this is real!" The mind, however, doesn't know the difference between reality or fantasy. We also don't have to put a lot of energy into it. There is no need to go out and actually do it; yet the incentive, the energy, and the need to act are gone.

AV: Finally, in the interview with O'Brien you stated your books "are trying to examine the disease . . . And the disease . . . is the lack of love." You then say your first four books only dealt with the problem, but that notes for forthcoming books would "incorporate the problem as well as the answer." Are you currently working on a new novel, and what can the reader look forward to from Hubert Selby, Jr.?

HS: Yes. I'm working on a new novel called *Seeds of Pain, Seeds of Love*. I'm three hundred pages into it. This is a creative effort to not only examine the problem, but to get from the problem to the answer. There is a little touch of that in some of the stories of *Song of the Silent Snow*, especially the title story, which is one of the last stories I've written. I hope this novel will succeed in the attempt to expand on the answer to the disease.

Yet this book is much different. My first four books examined the disease from a pathological perspective. I haven't been in any of my books. There is a difference now when I'm talking about the answer in this book, because most of the facts are facts from my life. I guess it could be considered autobiographical. Of course, you give a writer a fact and God only knows where you are going to end up. The basic facts are from my life, and, in addition to that, this book is written in the first person singular. Whether it will be totally that way or not, I don't know. It will be recognizable as being written by me because I seem to have a very distinctive style, or voice. I guess I'm one of those people who is more distinctive than others because of the nature and energy of my feelings as it is translated to my writing through my imagination. Hopefully, the seeds of my imagination will be productive.

Stroking the Sweet-Sour Depths

AN INTERVIEW WITH

Robert Stone

R OBERT S TONE was born in Brooklyn in 1937 to a father he never knew and a mother who was institutionalized for schizophrenia. He received a traditional Catholic high school education, which, despite his spirit of rebellion, gave him a grounding in the fundamentals of English and a love of literature.

Stone enlisted in the navy for three years, after which he returned to New York and attended NYU and worked as a copy boy for the *New York Daily News*.

His first novel, *Hall of Mirrors* (1967), is set in New Orleans and won the Faulkner Award. It was also made into the movie *WUSA*, starring Paul Newman. Stone's travels with Ken Kesey and the Merry Pranksters, along with a brief journalism stint in Vietnam, resulted in the highly praised novel *Dog Soldiers* (1974). The novel won the National Book Award for its portrayal of the effects of Vietnam and the drug culture on individuals. The author's screenplay of *Dog Soldiers* was made into the movie *Who'll Stop the Rain?* starring Nick Nolte. *A Flag for Sunrise* (1981) depicts America's involvement in Central America, while *Children of Light* (1986) is primarily set in Mexico and metaphorically showcases the malaise of the Hollywood film industry.

Robert Stone's novels invariably explore the darker side of mankind. As the critic A. Alvarez has stated, "In just four novels in almost twenty years Robert Stone has established a world and style and tone of voice of great originality and authority. It is a world without grace or comfort, bleak, dangerous, and continually threatening." Robert Stone's fifth novel is *Outerbridge Reach*, published in 1992.

The following interview took place on September 18, 1990, at the Wyndham Warwick Hotel in Houston, Texas. It was conducted shortly before Stone was to read at the Museum of Fine Arts. I recall going to his hotel room and being received by a man somewhat older (he was fifty-five at the time) than I expected. On the basis of my research, I also expected Stone to be more street-smart and tough-edged than he was. In the course of the interview, he was polite but quite reserved, and I was continually amazed at how gracefully and deliberately he spoke. It was obvious that words mattered, both written and spoken—and those words should be precise in their usage.

I also sensed that he was a writer with something to prove. Other writers might have been satisfied to win the National Book Award or have their novels made into movies, but I don't believe he was terribly enamored of the criticism and lack of attention that met the publication of his fourth novel, *Children of Light*. When I pressed him to discuss his work-in-progress (*Outerbridge Reach*), he resisted. Coincidentally, it was around this time that his voice started to weaken and crack as we approached the end of the interview. He decided it was best to stop so that he would not lose his voice before his speaking engagement that evening.

AV: When did you decide to become a writer?
RS: I wanted to be a writer from an early age. I had dropped out of high school and joined the navy when I was seventeen, and I think by the time I was eighteen or nineteen I knew I wanted to be a writer. I had always liked to write on some level, but I think what made me really decide to

become a professional writer was the experience I had in the navy during the late 1950s.

AV: Did your experience working as a journalist for the *New York Daily News* help you prepare to write fiction?

RS: I don't think there is any direct connection, but rather a lot of indirect connections. I started as a copy boy and also wrote sports captions, but I didn't do anything of any particular complication. I certainly didn't learn anything about writing while working at the *Daily News,* but I did have experiences in New York that were useful to me in the long run. I would like to add that I am not one of those people who think news writing is good training for a writer. I think the opposite.

AV: You stated in *Modern Fiction Studies* that you prefer fiction to journalism. Would you comment on this?

RS: I think I may have said that you don't have to be in a position to let the facts get in the way of truth. In fiction you order the illusion of continuity to suit a certain scheme when you have to deal with actual occurrences which are much more random and pointless. You then find yourself in the position of imposing a meaning. You might express it as discovering a meaning, but it is, in fact, imposing a meaning, and in this you're limited. You have this responsibility to be accurate, which, in a way, costs you in terms of essential truths. It's hard to be both perceptive and absolutely accurate. Fiction is something where you create the illusion of life, the illusion of continuity, and the illusion of cause and effect. That seems to me a freer way of working, and I find it more rewarding.

AV: Receiving the Stegner Fellowship in 1982 must have been a critical point in your life, because you moved to California and became involved with Ken Kesey and the Merry Pranksters. What was it like with Kesey, Cassady, Babbs, Mountain Girl, Owsley, and the rest of the Pranksters?

RS: I knew all those people, and I even rode on the bus with them—although not all the way across the country. I don't think anybody rode all the way across the country if they could help it. I've even used Cassady as a model for characters. It seems Cassady's fate in America is to be used as a model in so many different people's work. I used him after a fashion in a short story I wrote called "Porque No Tiene, Porque Le Falta," which is about a bunch of crazy American druggies in Mexico. It was in *The Best American Short Stories* of 1970, which was originally published in *New American Review #6*. The title is from the lyrics of a song called "La Cucaracha" that goes like this: "La Cucaracha, La Cucaracha/Ya no puede caminar/Porque no tiene, porque le falta/Marijuana par' fumar."

AV: Is Holliwell from *A Flag for Sunrise* based on Cassady or Kesey?

RS: No. Holliwell was certainly not anything like Cassady. Cassady was a guy of tremendous streetwiseness, but absolutely no education or cultivation except for what he picked up from Ginsberg or Kerouac or what he read in paperback books. He wasn't dumb, but he certainly wasn't intellectually sophisticated. Holliwell was a professor.

AV: What is your opinion of Cassady? You probably saw him a few years before he died in Mexico, didn't you?

RS: I saw him at his worst. I first met him in 1962 or 1963. He died in 1968 just before his forty-fourth birthday. He was a walking cautionary tale about speed. If you wanted to think of one hundred reasons not to take speed, then Cassady could provide you with at least eighty of them.

AV: You have also stated in *Modern Fiction Studies* that Dieter (from *Dog Soldiers*) is not based on Kesey, yet Dieter tells Marge that what he had experienced was something profound, "but rather difficult to verbalize." This seems to echo Tom Wolfe's *The Electric Kool-Aid Acid Test* where it says: "They made a point of not

putting it into words. That in itself was one of the un-
spoken rules." Perhaps you can comment on this since
Kesey, Wolfe, and you certainly make use of words.

RS: The thing is, that cult of ineffability that Wolfe is talking about is true of the Pranksters and of Cassady, but it
is also true of just about every single other romantic
avant-garde movement for the last one hundred and fifty
years. This harks back to the first German romantics and
the idea of what can't be verbalized and that which is
entirely intuitive. The '60s were an American expression
of an intellectual and artistic tradition that really is very
old. The only thing unique about them was their American aspect. Dieter is just a person of that time who is a
kind of spiritual adventurer, part charlatan, part genuine
mystic. He doesn't resemble Kesey in personality or style
of speech or even in action. He presided over a strange
scene, but you can probably find eight hundred guys who
presided over strange scenes in that period. He has things
in common with Kesey inasmuch as they both were
"gurus," as they used to say at that time, but they aren't
alike.

AV: It's interesting that people such as Kesey or Kerouac or
Cassady are often revered, but their real lives are not
what most people imagine. For example, Jack Kerouac
wrote *On the Road,* which is considered the Bible of
personal freedom and expression; yet, Kerouac dis-
avowed his status as the "Father of The Beats" or the
"Grandfather of the Hippies." He became an alcoholic
who was closer to being a redneck than a beatnik when
he died in 1969. I don't know what kind of commentary
this should elicit about the writer and the perpetration of
the romantic myth.

RS: In the case of Kerouac, he was an extremely romantic,
extremely sentimental, extremely sensitive individual. He
was an inheritor in the tradition of Whitman and of the
expanding American continent, which was a kind of mys-

ticism of the land. It's hard to remember, if you weren't around or if you are not a certain age, the kind of ridicule Kerouac was subject to in his own lifetime. He was very famous and influential, but he was constantly mocked for his writing that came out of the '50s. All the big publications and the national news magazines, in a way that would simply not occur today, treated him like a complete joke, like a boob, like a comedian, like a clown. This hurt him. He wasn't being taken seriously by anybody, whether it was the news media or even by the literary establishment; yet at the same time they were taking Ginsberg seriously. Kerouac was brutalized by the American media. He looked very strapping and strong, but his health had always been bad. He was insecure, and he didn't have much self-confidence, so he would be tremendously hurt by the kind of mockery the news media subjected him to, and he succumbed to drink. The rest of the story involves drugs when he became an anti-Semite and an ultra right-winger. I think this was alcoholic anger and a combination of spoiled romanticism whereby his early youthful enthusiasm was disappointed. He had a lot of quirks and psychological flaws, and he was stingy. He couldn't stand to give you a cigarette. He was very badly wounded by criticism and driven to alcoholism. The worse he felt, the more he drank; and the more he drank, the worse he felt. It became a vicious circle.

AV: I can see where you might identify with Kerouac—for example, by his upbringing and the fact that he was close to his mother. He also traveled extensively. I know your childhood was atypical. [Stone's parents never married; he never knew his father, who deserted the family. His mother lost her elementary school teaching job because of schizophrenia. He lived in various rooming houses and welfare hotels where his mother worked as a chambermaid. Raised a Catholic and educated by the Marist Brothers, he quit school before graduation after disgracing himself by drinking too much beer and being "militantly atheistic."] So, is Kerouac someone with whom you identified?

RS: I don't know if I identified with him, even though I was a teenager and a young sailor when he was a famous novelist. I admired him a lot and liked his work, but I find it pretty unreadable, to tell you the truth. I loved *On The Road*, although I'm not even sure why. I think because it just reached everyone who had that romance about American possibility and the American road. In a way, I don't think we're alike either as writers or as people. Our backgrounds, in some ways, are similar, and we are certainly touched by the same artistic, bohemian tradition that we shared, but not too much else.

AV: There is a kind of Kafkaesque atmosphere in bits of your writing that borders on the unreal, or surreal. Is this grounded in some kind of drug experience?

RS: I'm trying to replicate a state of mind, very often with the state of mind being a mixture of subjective things and objective things. I'm a realist as a writer in a very limited way. I'm trying to accurately portray emotional and psychological states, so they can be recognized. I think you have to go beyond the level of naturalism in order to do that. The only way you can make words evoke psychological and emotional states effectively is by creating an altered state of consciousness. My way of doing that is to write a lot of prose that is close to blank verse and is evocative in the same ways that poetry is. I'm certainly not a naturalist or a conventional realist. I'm after another kind of reality: the kind of reality that is subjectively experienced from the inside.

AV: "Robert Stone is the apostle of the strung-out" according to Jean Strouse during her review of *Children of Light* in the *New York Times Book Review*. Your characters are among the most difficult for a reader to identify with of any contemporary writer, with the possible exception of Hubert Selby, Jr. For example, Geraldine in *A Hall of Mirrors* seems to have the same mentality as Tralala in Selby's *Last Exit to Brooklyn,* as evidenced when Geraldine thinks to herself: "It would be hard to tell somebody, she thought, how you could come to hate a day like this. Because it was beautiful, by God, it was as beautiful as you could ever want. She felt a sudden urge to find the darkest end of the darkest rankest bar on Decatur Street and drink herself sodden."

Since many readers would have a hard time understanding or identifying with or even sympathizing with characters like Geraldine, what do you expect your readers to learn from them? Also—do you see any correlation between Selby's characters and your characters, since you both are from Brooklyn?

RS: There is not a writer I feel less in common with than Selby. His characters, it seems to me, have absolutely no inner life of any kind. What's going on with Geraldine in that particular scene is the fact that she is really moved by how nice a day it is and her capacity, her enjoyment of life, is considerable. It's her loss of happiness that she is lamenting because things haven't gone her way. She is unhappy. What the narrator is trying to convey is the force of her unhappiness. I can't even imagine associating the word "unhappy" or something as relatively uncomplicated a thing as unhappiness with a Selby character. I mean Geraldine has an inner life. She has an interiority, she has a mind, she has emotions, and she is capable of love. I've never read a character of Selby's who had any of these things or who had an inner life at all. You can't identify with Selby's characters, it seems to me, because there isn't a hell of a lot to them. It's like identifying with Raymond Chandler's characters where the other people are all monodimensional. So if people can't identify with my characters, there is nothing I can do.

AV: I didn't say readers can't identify with your characters, but that it may be hard to identify with them.

RS: I really think that what my characters go through is what most people go through at one time or another. It seems to me most people feel the way Geraldine feels in that one particular scene. People often feel betrayed by love. They feel let down or as though they are letting other people down. They have trouble with drugs and alcohol. But none of these things in my experiences are uncommon. If people don't identify with these characters and feel anything for them, then all I can say is they ought to.

AV: There is also a line from *A Hall of Mirrors*: "It's a great life if you don't weaken." This recalls the same line that appears in Alan Sillitoe's *Saturday Night and Sunday Morning*. Was this line taken from that novel?

RS: That line is taken from a contemporary country song by Roy Acuff, which goes something like this: "It's a great life if you don't weaken, but who wants to be strong?" I think it was on the boxes (juke box) when I was in the navy around 1960.

AV: I wonder if that song predates Sillitoe's book, which was published in 1958.

RS: I doubt if Sillitoe, being in England, would have heard that song, but I think that's probably a common phrase thrown around.

AV: What about your literary influences?

RS: I was influenced by Hemingway as a young reader. Hemingway made discoveries that were almost technical about how prose works, and I've used those as so many others have. Very much Joseph Conrad, a writer I tremendously admire, and a writer who is tremendously influential now. Conrad shows what a novel is supposed to be and how it can be made to work in novels like *Victory* and *Under Western Eyes*. *Victory* is one of my absolute favorites. John Dos Passos and F. Scott Fitzgerald are writers I read with great pleasure when I was young. I also admire Flaubert and Evelyn Waugh. My literary influences are really quite conventional in a literary way.

AV: You provided the text for the Vietnam photo textbook called *Images of War*. My wife, who is from Vietnam, was looking at the book and almost became sick because the graphic photos brought back so many bad memories. How did you manage to write the text?

RS: I have done a number of texts for books of photography, including one for James Nachtwey's book, which is called *Deeds of War: Photographs 1981 to 1988*. It's one of the best books of photographs I've ever seen. I think people ask me to write texts for the photo textbooks of Vietnam because I've written about Vietnam and I worked there in 1971. I wasn't there a terribly long time, but I've had certain adventures which to me were very important and they always stayed with me.

AV: I've read you spent less than two months in Vietnam; yet the text you wrote was very insightful. What was your experience in Vietnam and how did it shape your outlook?

RS: I spent a short time in Vietnam, but each day was different. It shaped my outlook on the United States in many complicated ways that keep changing. The idea of a mistake of that dimension was a very funny thing to see. If you were brought up as a kid during the war, you were used to an America which was always successful— and not just always successful, but totally and always in the right. Concerning the rights and wrongs of Vietnam, one can always go back and forth endlessly; certainly it was a miscalculation, in spite of whatever else it may have been. This was pretty easy to see. You didn't have to be terribly astute: the size of the thing, the tremendous dimensions, the number of people, the number of installations, the amount of material—you knew right away this was all wrong. It was all misapplied. It was a mistake. This gigantic 10,000-mile mistake was very jarring to see. I never saw a single act that I found to be utterly inhuman. It was a sustained war, being very different from what most people imagined. We have the impression that the war fought in Europe during World War II was fought in a completely different way than Vietnam. The common belief is that civilians in Europe were universally spared and never got blown up or never got burned with jelly gasoline. In fact, this happened all the time. An enormous number of French, Dutch, German, and even Danish civilians were killed by Allied forces. I didn't see any atrocities or egregious acts of cruelty. What I did see was this ongoing process, this kind of blinker-vision, go-ahead, can-do spirit. It told me something about the American can-do spirit and the idea about America which refuses to make choices and refuses to admit to the limits of its power, which is going on still today. I react to this, not because I think it's essentially morally wrong, although it often puts us there; I react to it as an American, as a patriot, as a taxpayer. This was a revelation to me. What I saw in Vietnam was this hubris, this over-confidence, this refusal to think in human terms about an enemy or about a situation. A war is an utterly human situation. Yet we treated it entirely as a technical problem. It was, in fact, a conflict between human beings, and we made it everything but that. This may not be answering your question, but in another way it is. We just absolutely declined to realize that this was a hassle between human beings. We treated it as though it were an entirely technical problem, as if we were trying to build a skyscraper, when we were actually involved in a contest of wills with people we never tried to understand.

Let me give you an example. Frances Fitzgerald tells the story about her father, Desmond Fitzgerald, who is a

CIA man. One day he had the job of briefing Robert McNamara who was Secretary of Defense. The CIA always had to brief McNamara a couple of times a week, and you always had to bring your visual aides because McNamara wanted everything quantified. The guys in the Pentagon, the Kennedy whiz kids who went on to work for Johnson, they had it worked out *statistically* with graphs. There was no way the war could be lost. No possible rate of attrition could keep the United States from prevailing. It was all on the charts.

Then one day, Desmond Fitzgerald went over for the briefing and he didn't bring any charts or any numbers at all. McNamara sat through his briefing and then said to Mr. Fitzgerald, "Where are your visual aides? Where are the figures?" And Fitzgerald said, in effect, "Well, look, sometimes you just have to get out in the hills and walk around, ride the buses, go to the fruit market, listen to what people are saying, pick up on the gossip, and try to find out what's going on. Sometimes that's much more important than anything you could put on a chart." McNamara said, "Thank you very much, Mr. Fitzgerald," and then he said to his deputy, "I never want to see that man in this office again." *He wanted numbers.* He was a numbers man. The military establishment continues to be technically oriented, in a way that almost makes it unable to think. They can reason mechanically, but they can't exactly think.

AV: It's almost like the U.S. military mind is like that of a robot.

RS: It's a robotic consciousness. It's a nonverbal and almost a nonhuman consciousness, which is not to say that these people are somehow like robots or that they are not human. The intelligence that they have created is robotic and nonhuman. There is no way we can figure out exactly how much the Iranians hate us. We say Iran's motives have to be economically determined or that they won't cooperate with the Iraqis. We have no way of making the machine think. There are elements in Iran that hate us so much that they will endure any amount of deprivation and even go directly against their obvious interests in order to hurt us. We can't do that kind of thinking. We can figure out exactly how to hurt them economically and militarily, but we can't do the other stuff. This is one of the reasons why we couldn't function in Vietnam. We had no declared ends, except we were trying to fight a political war in utterly nonpolitical ways because our guys were all apolitical technocrats. They didn't want to pay any attention to the political dimension of it. The only dimension they had was one-dimensional.

AV: Too bad we didn't learn from the French, who were probably laughing at us the whole time.

RS: The French were laughing at us because they never believed we were trying to help them, and they didn't want us to succeed where they failed.

AV: Incidentally, on page 141 of *Images of War,* there is a picture of a man in a wheelchair who looks like Ron Kovic who wrote the book *Born on the Fourth of July* that was later made into a movie of the same name. Is that Ron Kovic?

RS: My first response was to say no, but after looking at the photo it might be.

AV: Do you think winning the National Book Award for *Dog Soldiers* in 1975 increased expectations from critics and therefore increased the pressure on you as a writer? Do you think there was any harm in winning that prize so early in your career?

RS: The pressure is always going to be there, and the expectations ought to be high. You should always be trying to learn. No matter what you are doing, you should always be trying to do it better.

I have no regrets about the award. I want the critics'

expectations to be high. I don't expect to be let off easy, and I don't want to be let off easy by the critics. Not that I think the critics are always right or that they are always perceptive.

AV: You used a passage from Conrad's *Heart of Darkness* as an epigraph to open *Dog Soldiers*, and you have already said that Conrad was an influence. Why has this book of Conrad's been such a popular literary yardstick for Vietnam stories? For example, the movie *Apocalypse Now* was loosely based on *Heart of Darkness*, even though Conrad was writing about Africa.

RS: Conrad was a chronicler of late imperial ironies. Vietnam was a situation he would have immediately understood. People in Vietnam were in a Conradian situation. They were in the same kind of trouble as Kurtz was or Baron Axel Heyst was in *Victory*. There are great similarities between late imperial England that Conrad was writing about and the American condition at the time of the Vietnam War.

AV: Correct me if I'm wrong, but your style recalls language used by such writers as Somerset Maugham and Oscar Wilde. For example, in *Dog Soldiers* you state: "In Converse's view, the idea of a Korean soldier reading a *Zap* comic was worth the loss of the case." Or, when Ian Percy is preaching to Converse, he says: "Why don't you go watch some other place die? They've got corpses by the river-full in Bangle Desh. Why not go there?" Whereupon Converse replies, "It's dry." How did you acquire this style of subtle wit and sarcasm?

RS: It's my natural style.

AV: There are several references to Satan throughout *Dog Soldiers* as well as references to angelic images, including the missionary lady who tells Converse that people who don't believe in Satan "are in for an unpleasant surprise." Do you think Satan, metaphorically speaking, lived in Vietnam?

RS: I think Satan is everywhere there are people. This is an aspect of people who are weak and short-sighted and enraged. This is where Satan is, wherever that is going on, and that is always going on somewhere.

The view I have of the world—which is reflected in *Dog Soldiers* and probably in all my books—is essentially a religious one in structure. It doesn't necessarily attach to any body of creed, but the world to me is structured in a kind of religious way. The metaphor of religion that is embodied in the tradition of Christianity is to me a very useful one for addressing the moral problems of the world. My schema, my parameters for dealing with the world and people, is essentially a religious one and the terms in which I tend to think are religious terms.

AV: Converse changes the Descartian argument to "I am afraid, therefore I am." Yet the fear in *Dog Soldiers* seems to be sublimated by too much death and too many drugs.

RS: Converse has a very hard time of it. What he is about is perception. He is a subject of fear who is in very frightening circumstances. What I'm saying is only that and really nothing more. I'm not making any broad philosophical point. I'm just saying this is a guy who found himself pursuing a couple of exotic impulses in a very frightening situation.

AV: Drugs play a significant role throughout much of your fiction. What role did drugs play in your formative years as a writer?

RS: I never became addicted to drugs. I don't think drugs particularly interfered with my life. Obviously, around the electric scene described in *The Electric Kool-Aid Acid Test* drugs were taken. I don't know how different my writing would be without drugs. I certainly don't write in a state of intoxication of any kind. I do not take drugs or drink in order to write. I don't write stoned in any way.

AV: Yet you wrote a very convincing and powerful scene at the end of *Dog Soldiers*, after Hicks has shot up with heroin and is walking along the railroad tracks and the landscape around him is almost surreal. How did you write this scene so convincingly?

RS: It's really more about heat and pain than it is about drugs. If you know something about drugs, you ought to know something about how drugs work to write that scene. The reason he shot up with heroin was to kill the pain after being severely wounded.

AV: Do you feel any affinity with William Burroughs and such books as *Junkie* and *Naked Lunch*?

RS: Affinity is not exactly the word. What I admire in those works of Burroughs is their humor. I think that humor is essentially a humane and moral impulse. I admire the fact that Burroughs goes into this world of utter freakishness—a kind of nonhuman, brutal, and amoral world of freakishness—and introduces a certain humor which I think is humane and wholesome. But other than that, affinity is not quite the word. There is a lot in Burroughs I have no affinity for, but I do like his black humor.

AV: Did you know that the cyberpunk science fiction writers such as William Gibson consider both you and Burroughs as distinct influences for their genre?

RS: I hadn't heard that before, but I'm glad to hear it.

AV: There is an interesting passage that describes Hicks making love to Converse's wife:

> Because of his nature and circumstances, the most satisfying part of Hicks' sexual life had come to be masturbation—he preferred it to prostitutes because it was more sanitary and took less time. He did not take it lightly when, rarely, one woman pleased him, and his deepest pleasures were intellectual and emotional. He became a hoarder, careful and slow to the point of obsessiveness, a thinker.
>
> He eased towards the light, his strength in his tongue, stroking the sweet-sour depths and surfaces. When he was ready he went in, striking for the deepest darkest part of her the limits of himself could reach, then eased up, stirring, stroking from inside. She came and spoke to him; he thought she said, "Find thee."

I found these two paragraphs very expressive, and, yet, Hicks is trying to intellectualize sex, which is pretty hard to do. Phrases such as "stroking the sweet-sour depths" are so wonderfully descriptive.

RS: I think what one is trying to do in art is to provide a recognition. You are trying to create an experience for your audience, but you create an experience by leading them to recognition of something they already know. That makes the process—of reading, or looking at the picture, or whatever they're doing—a living, active process. So this "stroking the sweet-sour depths" passage is meant to lead people to recognition because everybody knows what that means. All I am trying to do is lead people to the recognition of something they already know. It just lights up the moment, and they know exactly where the character is.

AV: What about the words "Find thee?"

RS: It's from a line that's in the "Wreck of the Deutschland" by Gerard Manley Hopkins. I think the line goes, "Feel thy finger and find thee."

AV: There are interesting passages about existence in *Dog Soldiers*. The first passage is from Converse's insight on fragmentation bombing in Vietnam: "One insight was that the ordinary physical world through which one shuffled heedless and half-assed toward non-entity was capable of composing itself at any time and without notice, into a massive instrument of agonizing death. Existence was a trap; the testy patience of things as they are might be exhausted at any moment."

Can you comment on your views of existence or existentialism? Also, does being removed from war make one less cognizant of one's mortality?

RS: I think being away from danger and from pressure—or maybe it works the other way around when you see a lot of physical annihilation close at hand—your own mortality occurs to you more vividly and more pertinently.

As far as philosophical views go, I think the great existential novelist is Dostoyevsky.

The fact that we have to impose meaning on a seemingly random and meaningless universe is something I share with most people. I think most people believe this in one form or another. I do believe in a moral dimension. I believe that nothing is free. I believe you always have to pay off one end or the other. I think there is a traditionally historical philosophy at the core of my system of beliefs. I think existentialism has become so much a truism that you can hardly speak of existentialism because we are all existentialists now.

AV: I find a dichotomy between the two: the intelligent world is probably viewing things from an existentialist viewpoint about the meaning of life, if there is any, and yet we are still living in a religious house. It is interesting how you manage to combine those two elements.

RS: I think it was Paul Tillich who spoke about God as a dynamic absence: if God is not, it doesn't necessarily change the way things are. Instead of a dynamic presence there is dynamic absence. You don't necessarily have to have an extra-personal God to have a religious framework. You can have a religious framework that doesn't have God in it. In this case it can become an absolutely dynamic and highly significant absence or a kind of vacuum that blends absurdity to the human action. Those two things don't contradict each other. You don't have to be a Deist to see things in a religious framework.

AV: There is frequent mention throughout your fiction of moral issues. For example, in *Dog Soldiers* there is a conversation: "Aren't there some funny moral areas here?" Jody asks, and Margie responds, "I guess it depends on your sense of humor." Do you subscribe to John Gardner's premise from his book *On Moral Fiction* that fiction should have a moral point of view?

RS: I think it has to. We can't help having one. That's the

nature of language because you are always making choices, you are always presenting options. Fiction has an inescapable moral connection. There is just no way around it. You are always presenting things in a favorable or unfavorable light. You are always making judgments.

AV: Would you align yourself with such writers as John Gardner and John Fowles rather than William Gass, John Barth, and Thomas Pynchon?

RS: Yes.

AV: Tom Wolfe has recently written a controversial essay called "Stalking the Billion-Footed Beast." What are your thoughts about Wolfe's essay, which many critics have found to be self-serving?

RS: I have a lot of admiration for Tom Wolfe. I think he's a very good writer. When he was a young writer, the realism-naturalism character appeared to be passé while writers like Barth, Hawkes, Gass, and Coover—who I wouldn't put in quite the same category—were popular and whose characters or fiction often evoked a kind of nonrealism.

I think American realism, although not traditional realism, has made a tremendous comeback. Wolfe writes as though he is still going against the prevailing grain in writing a realistic novel, but that simply is not so nowadays. It was when he began to write in the early '60s when *Giles Goat-Boy* and *The Sot-Weed Factor* were the big important books of the time, but those days are long gone. We've had an entire generation of young realist writers like Raymond Carver and Tobias Wolffe and many others too numerous to mention.

AV: You mentioned two novels by Barth that some critics consider classics. Yet you are saying those books are no longer as important as they were.

RS: I don't mean to say those works are no longer important. I'm just saying they are not the dominant mode now. Yet, Tom Wolfe is somehow writing that these fabulist works of fiction are still the dominant mode in American fiction, which isn't the case. The dominant mode in fiction is realist writers like Bobbie Ann Mason, Margaret Atwood, and Richard Ford, and so forth. Tom Wolfe is not rebelling against the dominant mode anymore. Maybe he was in the past, but he is not now.

AV: Can you explain the following items from *Dog Soldiers:* the name Antheil; "stone the gash"; Those Who Are; and A.M.D.G.?

RS: There was an American composer in Paris in the 1920s named George Antheil who was a prolific composer. He wrote *Ballet Mécanique* and later went on to write movies. I like the name "Antheil" because it suggests fascism and insects.

"Stone the gash" means get the woman high. "Gash" is an extremely vulgar term for a woman.

"Those Who Are" is an old Greek Homeric term. Hicks has the Greek letters tattooed on his arm and it has to do with Hicks' sense of who he is and a kind of secret society.

A.M.D.G. is the motto of the Jesuits. *Ad majorem Dei gloriam* are the Latin words, which translate "to the greater glory of God." Those letters are inscribed over the gateway to Dieter's ranch.

AV: You wrote the screenplays for *WUSA* starring Paul Newman, based on *A Hall of Mirrors*, and also *Who'll Stop the Rain?* starring Nick Nolte, based on *Dog Soldiers*. Yet, you have expressed reservations about the finished product.

RS: I think you lose a lot when you make a book into a movie, because you lose the open-endedness and you cut off possibilities. With literature, there are many possibilities where words can cast a certain shadow, whereas, with film, you are absolutely limited to only one order of appearances. So the imagination can't run free. It's determined by what the eyes see.

There is also a way in which movies tend to resist moral ambiguities, which are the principle subjects of my work. Movies don't like my ambiguities. Movies really compel you to decide if this is a good person or a bad person. It's almost the nature of moving-picture photography. You are always leading people to essentially simple judgments, and it is very hard to portray a lot of ambiguity.

AV: I think one exception would be Hitchcock's *Psycho*, where the audience is trying to identify with this woman who has embezzled some money and halfway through the movie she is murdered. I think the reader of *Dog Soldiers* experiences the same thing by trying to identify with Converse, but halfway through the novel Converse's wife takes off with the so-called paranoid psychopath Hicks. Perhaps if Hitchcock were still alive, he could have done justice to your novel.

RS: You can't have two things to deal with at once about a character in a movie. It's hard to get people in a movie to think that something is awful and funny at the same time. I'm not saying movies can't handle this, but it is much harder for a film to achieve.

AV: Such characters as Rheinhardt, Converse, Hicks, Holliwell, and Walker in your novels seem to share a fundamental inability to face reality, with their perceptions further distorted by drugs or alcohol.

RS: I don't think they are unable to "face reality." I think, in fact, their specialty is perception. They are constantly identifying and defining the nature of the action of reality in an extremely intense and perceptive way. It's not that these men can't face reality; it's that they confront it all too well. They confront it all too vigorously and intensely all the time.

AV: Can you see any of these characters, who are using drugs or alcohol, where they might progress to the point of facing reality?

RS: It depends what you mean by "facing reality." What

does it mean to face reality? Does it mean not thinking about how things are? There are very few people I know who have moved to a situation where they "face reality." As in the psycho-babble phrase, one can take "control of their lives" and can make their lives less chaotic. The trouble with my characters is that they are adventurers. They are pursuing sensation. They are pursuing more life. They are also victims of spite. These people are not so much avoiding reality as they are reacting with spite to the dissatisfactions of life which they experience. Ahab, in *Moby Dick,* is acting in a tremendously spiteful way.

So one can say this character's behavior is adolescent or immature, but it is also universally human. My characters are not missing some point, because they actually understand the situation correctly. It's their actions they cannot bring to bear because there is no completely satisfying moral ground for them to stand on. They have all lived examined lives. They all have highly developed moral sensibilities. They act against their own better instincts out of the necessities of the moment. They let each other down because of the situations they have gotten themselves into. They are not missing some point, as I have said, because they are involved in life in a very real way. The world they are seeing is quite clear; it does exist.

AV: Despite being on opposite sides of the law, Hicks and Danskin don't appear to be much different. In fact, I would say Hicks is a much better person—much more moral, and substantially saner than Danskin.

RS: That is the intention. Danskin is a smart, articulate psychopath. He is a true psychopath who has poor instincts. Hicks, despite what Converse thinks, is not a psychopath, while having very good instincts.

AV: What about the process of an interview? Does it help you when you try to verbalize your thoughts about fiction?

RS: Yes, it really does.

AV: The interview also allows the reader to get a better understanding of the writer.

RS: People don't understand that a writer is an illusionist, a performer. You don't expect an actor to be as crazy as his performance, and writing is performance. It is art. It is storytelling. Very few writers are the kind of creatures one might encounter in their books.

AV: Several critics were not very receptive to *Children of Light* because they said you were essentially reworking old themes, but in different settings.

RS: It seems to me *Children of Light* and *A Flag for Sunrise* are very different books. I can't imagine someone reading *Children of Light* and saying this is like *A Flag for Sunrise*. I don't know what they mean by that. If they mean heterosexual love and people's capacity for not coming through for each other, then those things are similar. I think the styles in the books are very different.

AV: What can readers expect in your latest novel, *Outerbridge Reach*?

RS: It has a lot of sailing in it. I don't want to say too much, but readers have a right to insight and poetry. That's what I'm trying to do.